10
FITNESS

100%
FITNESS

James and Leona Hart

RIGHT WAY

Printed and bound in Great Britain by
Cox & Wyman Ltd, Reading, Berkshire.

Published by Elliot Right Way Books, Brighton Road,
Lower Kingswood, Tadworth, Surrey, KT20 6TD, U.K.

CONTENTS

INTRODUCTION

There are increasing numbers of men and women who, without wanting to be involved in any particular sport or game, are nevertheless concerned to maintain or improve their levels of physical fitness through some form of personal exercise programme.

But what is fitness? Is there a special point at which you can be considered physically fit?

Jogging and running are popular at the moment, although many other kinds of activities, such as cycling, swimming, aerobics etc., also have their enthusiasts.

But how do such activities compare for general fitness training? Have you got to do some kind of running to be fit? And if so, what kind?

Again, weight training is steadily increasing in popularity, among both men and women, and various different forms of weight training equipment are also becoming much more widely available.

But is weight training a good method for improving fitness? What is the best kind of apparatus for weight training?

There are also the committed sports people and games players who wish to become fitter in order to perform or to play better.

What aspects of fitness should be developed, and what are the appropriate types of training? Is a 5 mile jog useful to a footballer or a rugby player? Would increased strength benefit, or be harmful to, performance? What is the best way of improving strength?

This book attempts to provide answers to these and other questions in this area. It describes the range of attributes that contribute to fitness, and shows how different forms of training develop quite different components of fitness. Methods of using the key training activities of running, circuit training and weight training are described in detail. Advice is given on aspects of nutrition and diet, and also on how to handle and respond to injuries. Besides simply giving a greater awareness of the scope of physical fitness, the book should enable any individual, who is interested in improving his or her general fitness, to construct an appropriate programme of activity. And it should also help the serious games player to match the appropriate types of training to the required components of fitness – or even to abandon inappropriate types of training!

1

BACKGROUND TO FITNESS AND TRAINING

What Is Physical Fitness?

When asked to think of a physically fit individual, what sort of image comes to mind? Not surprisingly perhaps, it may be of a particular sports champion since success in physical activity must imply a high degree of fitness – but which champion and which sport? Would it be a world-class runner, or does the greater all-round athleticism of a decathlete mean greater fitness? Is a champion weight-lifter likely to be less fit than a swimmer? And what about the fitness of a racing driver?

The first point is that different sports have quite different requirements, and even among top-class performers from these sports, all of whom must be extremely fit, there is no obvious single characteristic of physical fitness. However, a clue to the nature of fitness lies, not in the particular activities themselves, but in the fact that, when asked to describe an individual who is fit, we probably think of some actual champion. That is, *'fitness' is simply the ability to carry out some particular activity; 'getting fitter' means being able to do it better; and being 'very fit' means being able to do it better than anyone else*. This is more or less the best notion of fitness that physical educationists have come up with: all concepts, and measures, of fitness are related to the level of performance in some chosen (and somewhat arbitrary) task. It therefore includes several different components, which are emphasised to different degrees in different sports.

A second general point concerns the obvious differences in build and appearance among the participants in different sports (particularly at champion level), and the extents to which these differences are either inherited or are developed by the sports themselves. We shall see that many elements of fitness certainly have strong genetic or inherited aspects.

These aspects become more and more important at the highest levels of performance and competition – indeed, there is some truth in the saying that to become a champion, you must choose your parents carefully. However, this is not to deny the requirements for hard work and training. Genetic background or inheritance determines only the potential level of performance; training determines the extent to which this potential is actually realised. A fully-trained individual will usually beat one who is less well-trained, even though the latter has greater ability.

The components of fitness and their general training

There are generally six attributes or characteristics involved in the expression of any physical activity:

skill
strength
speed
suppleness
stamina
skinniness.

These are the components that are used to different extents in different sports, and together they make up the total range of physical fitness. (The sixth component, skinniness or per-cent body fat, is not directly involved in activity, but its level affects the degree to which the others can be expressed and it is thus an important aspect of fitness.)

Before individual discussion of these components, two general points should be made. The first concerns the fact that all these words that describe aspects of fitness begin with 's'; this is a bit artificial, and is simply a deliberate memory aid. Secondly and more importantly, separate discussion of each component may give the misleading impression that they are independent. In fact, they are highly inter-related. For example, repetitive activity like running not only develops stamina, but also requires a certain amount of strength in the leg muscles; again, developing a muscle's strength also has a positive effect on the speed with which it can move a limb. However, besides such positive effects, there are also negative interactions between some components; prolonged stamina training can have harmful effects on both suppleness and speed.

Skill

The word 'skill' implies proficiency in some activity or other, and coaches and laymen alike recognise that physical (or motor) skill is an important aspect in virtually every sport. However, the word can be used in a number of different ways. A sportsman may use it to refer to the quality of a performance ("he played a skilful game"), or to the degree of difficulty in a particular sport ("ice hockey seems a skilful game"). In both of these cases, the word is being used to describe a task that is itself made up of many individual activities or movements. On the other hand, a motor learning psychologist, a person who actually studies skill, uses the word to refer to a single type of movement. This makes it possible to study skill, and in particular the acquisition of skill, in a more scientific fashion, since a complex activity is broken down into a series of specific movements, each of which can be described and measured. In this sense then, a skill is highly specific – there must be as many skills as there are different types of movement. Each physical skill is based upon a particular sequence of muscular events that occur in response to particular signals from the outside world (in sport, these are usually visual signals reinforced by sound, touch etc.). An awareness of the 'particularness' or individuality of skills is important when it comes to practising actual sports' skills.

(Another word used in this area is 'ability'. Some authorities consider that an ability is a more general trait that enables an individual to perform well in a number of related activities. Other authorities question the existence of such attributes. If they do exist, they are reckoned to be largely inherited or acquired in the first years of life.)

Skill training. Skill is a highly trainable aspect of fitness. Since the field of motor learning psychology virtually defines a skill as a learned movement, it follows that its performance can be improved with practice. However, for training to be effective, two conditions must be satisfied: there must be sufficient practice, and it must be appropriate practice. Questions as to what is sufficient practice are easily answered. Skill continues to improve almost indefinitely – any levelling off in performance is likely to be due to a decline in actual practice time or in motivation. Questions about the appropriateness of practice for particular skills involve aspects of skill specificity. In this respect, there are certain training principles that apply to skill practice for all sports and activities.

Principles of skill training:
1. *Skill training should be specific.* In fact, the most effective form of skill training is rehearsal of the actual activity itself. The extent to which proficiency in one skill influences performance in another is referred to as skill transferability, and it depends not only on the relatedness of the skills, but also on the proficiency of the performer. For example, tennis and squash could be expected to have a fair degree of transferability, and a beginner may be helped to develop basic strokes and strategies by playing both games. But a player who is skilled in one of the games may at first be confused by the differences in speed, stroke and position of the other game. Therefore, the practice of seemingly related skills should be avoided, especially by skilled performers. It is also inefficient to train with, say, a heavier club or racquet in the mistaken belief that this type of strength training will improve skill; timing and other skill factors are more likely to deteriorate.

2. *Complex skills can be practised as individual movements.* This method allows greater specificity to be achieved in the practice of the required movements, and also results in more effective feedback of information on the level of performance in each movement. Eventually, of course, the complete activity must be rehearsed.

3. *Feedback of information is important.* An individual practising a skill must know two things – exactly what is required in the movements, and the extent to which his or her performance actually achieves this. And the sooner such information is received, the more effective it is. (In this respect, video equipment enables a performer to observe and correct individual movements within a single training session.)

4. *The length of the practice session is significant.* Short sessions distributed over a period of time are generally more effective, and result in better skill retention, than longer sessions, even when the total lengths of time spent practising are similar.

Strength
This is the capacity to overcome resistance in a single, muscular effort, and it can be shown in different ways:

static strength involves isometric resistance against a stationary load, most obvious in holding a weight in a fixed position or in a rugby scrum;

dynamic strength uses isotonic contractions actually to move a load or lift a weight;

explosive strength describes the very fast muscular actions required of, for example, sprinters and jumpers.

(The meanings of the terms isometric and isotonic are explained in the section on how muscles work, in Chapter 3, page 96.) Strength is not determined by just a single physical characteristic. The raw motive power of muscle is transformed into effective strength only when it pulls against a bone lever. An individual's strength thus results from the interaction between non-muscle and muscle-based features.

Limb length is one of the most significant of the non-muscle factors. In the particular type of lever system that operates at most of the body joints, a long lever arm lessens the efficiency of leverage since the weight being lifted is further away from the joint pivot and the power source. Simply, an individual with long limbs will be 'less strong' than one with shorter limbs even though both can exert similar forces of muscular contraction (see Fig. 1). Less obvious aspects, such as the way in which the muscle is actually attached to its bone, can also influence the effective length of the bone lever.

Muscle size is probably the feature that is most popularly considered to determine strength. However, visible muscle bulk is not a reliable indicator of muscle strength since such bulk can be due to non-contractile (i.e. non-power-providing) connective tissues. (In fact, a significant part of the muscle bulk of body-builders is due to increased blood and blood vessels in the muscle, deliberately induced by their 'pumping' methods of training.) The size of the actual muscle tissue is made up of two components – the number of fibres within a muscle, and the thickness of the individual fibres themselves. Each of these aspects, fibre number and thickness, can be very different in the muscles of different people. Muscle fibre type is also important in determining the force that can be achieved in a single muscular contraction; so-called 'fast twitch' white muscle fibres (explained more fully in Chapter 3) are thicker and are more capable of contracting simultaneously, and thus of generating greater force, than are the 'slow twitch' red fibres. The proportions of these different fibre

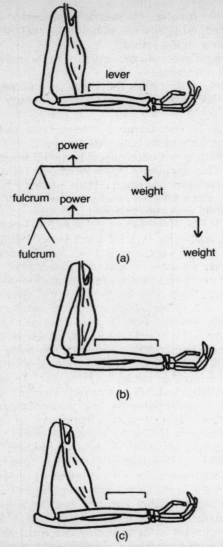

Fig. 1 Effects of limb length and efficiency of leverage on effective muscle power.
(a) Longer lever – less effective power action.
(b) Muscle attached close to the joint, long lever, poor efficiency.
(c) Muscle attached further from joint, shorter lever, higher efficiency.

types seem to vary greatly between different individuals.

A third category or factor also contributes force to a movement. This is termed the *elastic component* of strength, and it originates from the elastic properties of the tendons that connect muscles to bone and of the connective tissues that surround the bundles of fibres inside the muscle. It is a particularly important aspect of explosive strength and its effects can be seen by comparing a jump which has a preliminary bounce, with a jump from a static position; the sudden pre-stretch of the muscle in the initial bounce feeds 'elastic energy' into the connective tissues, and this contributes greater force to the contraction that immediately follows.

Finally, during normal activity a muscle is constantly changing in length as a consequence of its contraction and relaxation, and it can generate substantially different amounts of force at these different lengths, a feature referred to as the *power curve* of the muscle (its explanation is given in Chapter 3, page 97). The existence of this muscle power curve, together with the changing efficiency of leverage as a limb moves and the joint angles change, also means that markedly different levels of strength can be exerted at different limb positions.

Strength training. Only some of the elements that contribute to strength are affected by training. Several of the non-muscle factors can be developed to a limited degree. For example, the bones and the connective tissues of tendons and ligaments become thicker and stronger, and such changes have a positive effect on the elastic component of strength. But of all the non-muscle factors, limb length exerts the greatest influence on the effectiveness of muscle action, and this of course cannot be changed by training. Most of the muscle factors are also largely determined by inheritance, e.g. the number of fibres in a muscle. The extent to which training may increase the capacity to use more of the fibres in a muscle is somewhat uncertain, although there are suggestions that the ability to synchronise fibre activity can increase, and this must be an important aspect of dynamic strength movements. However, by far the largest and most significant effect of strength training on a muscle is an increase in the thickness of the muscle fibres. (Of course, the final size of each fibre, and of the muscle itself, is ultimately limited by factors of inheritance.)

Although the effects of strength training are thus limited to only a few components, considerable improvements in strength are possible for most people; an ordinary individual can expect to double his or her strength within six months of starting training. And such increases in strength may or may not, depending on details of diet and inheritance, be accompanied by a visible increase in muscle size.

The basic principles that govern any approach to strength training are outlined here (details of actual training programmes are given in Chapter 2).

Principles of strength training:

1. The maximum number of muscle fibres must be recruited. The main aim in all forms of strength training is to force the muscle to recruit as many of its fibres as possible during single contractions. If the maximum number of fibres is being used, the muscle is forced to adapt by increasing the thickness of the individual fibres. The major implication of this principle is that simply repeating a movement without any effort does not improve strength.

2. Maximum fibre recruitment occurs near the point of muscle failure. That is, the muscle only calls upon all its available fibres just as it is beginning to be overcome by the load it is acting against. However, simply repeating an exercise to the point of muscle failure is not necessarily an effective way to develop strength; if the load is such that only a small proportion of the total number of fibres needs to be recruited in each contraction, then only a proportion of the fibres is being 'trained' (stimulated to thicken) at any one time.

3. Different systems try to achieve maximum fibre recruitment in different ways. The actual means by which maximum fibre recruitment is best achieved is the subject of much debate, and various approaches have been developed. These are to a large extent based around different forms of muscle contraction, and often use different types of equipment.

Isometric systems: It is generally reckoned that isometric contractions (see page 96) result in maximum fibre recruitment. Isometric exercises involve holding the strongest possible contraction against an immovable load for 3–6 seconds. However, such systems have declined in popularity since they develop maximum force (and therefore strength?) in only one fixed position. (They also have no spin-off effects on other aspects of fitness, such as endurance or flexibility.)

Isotonic systems: Traditional methods of strength training use normal isotonic contractions in exercises with free weights. They involve carrying out repeated movements with a weight that is large enough to recruit an appropriate number of fibres; as the muscle tires during the repetitions, more fibres are recruited. What actually constitutes a 'large enough' weight is still fairly questionable and various patterns of loading and exercise repetition can be used (see the section on weight training in Chapter 2, page 61). However, free weights act as a constant resistance throughout any one movement, whereas the amount of force that can be generated by a muscle actually varies throughout the range of a movement (due to the muscle power curve). This means that in exercises with free weights, the muscle is either over-loaded at the extremes of the movement or sub-loaded in the middle range, and for this reason many authorities consider that isotonic systems cannot fully develop a muscle throughout its full range of action.

Training machines: In attempts to take account of the muscle power curve, some types of modern strength training equipment are designed so that the resistance, against which the muscle is working, actually varies throughout the range of any one movement. In *isokinetic machines* there is a fixed speed at which the exercise levers can be moved, automatically adjusting to the strength of the muscle. A similar sort of effect is achieved by working against hydraulic pistons, as in certain types of rowing machine; in these, the more vigorous the movement, the greater the hydraulic resistance. In *variable resistance machines* the actual load is varied by the machine itself. There are two popular examples of this type of machine: in the Universal multigym, the resistance is altered during certain movements by a changing machine leverage; in Nautilus machines, the exercise movement rotates a cam which changes the resistance in a manner designed to match the power curve of the muscle being exercised.

An increase in strength usually results in an improved performance in most sports, and many sportsmen and women nowadays include strength training in their programmes. Nevertheless, some people are still hesitant about starting such training because of fears of harmful effects on other aspects of their performance, or on their actual appearance. These fears are usually based upon one or more misconceptions about strength training.

Misconceptions about strength training:

1. Strength training develops large muscles. No. The massive development of a bodybuilder is due to a combination of inheritance, particular training methods and special nutrition. Similarly, the outstanding strength of the competitive weight-lifter owes a great deal to genetic potential, but it is not often accompanied by massive muscularity. The point is that there are quite different training methods for developing muscle size in particular, or for developing strength; and in both cases, the highest levels of proficiency owe as much to genes as to training. For most individuals, a doubling of strength will not be accompanied by a doubling in muscle size.

2. Strength training makes females look muscular. No. Everything said above is equally true for females, with the addition that the body composition and hormonal complement of most females are also not suited to muscular development. (Females are perfectly capable, however, of doing the same types and intensities of training as males – they just won't end up looking the same.)

3. Strength training makes you stiff and muscle bound. No (or maybe, if done wrongly). All forms of training should be accompanied by some form of stretching programme. In addition, exercise should be performed through the full range of a limb's movement, and this will actually improve suppleness. The extreme flexibility of competitive weight-lifters, particularly in the ankles, hips and shoulders, indicates that strength training in itself does not lead to stiffness. And the suppleness of even fairly bulky male gymnasts demonstrates that muscle bulk need not interfere with flexibility.

4. Muscles turn into fat when training stops. No. Muscle and fat are two quite separate types of tissues, and are not at all inter-convertible. This aspect is discussed further in the section on skinniness, page 26.

Speed

The meaning of this term is not restricted simply to the act of running fast, although that is certainly one aspect of it. In the general context of fitness, speed covers the capacities for all sorts of fast movements, and it is seen in the explosive actions of jumpers and weight-lifters as well as in the perhaps more obviously fast performances of, say, table tennis players. A high degree of speed is also useful in many other sports, not just for fast movement but for giving power to movement. (Power = speed × strength. Power can thus be increased by improvement in either component; many sprinters do a lot of strength training, while weight-lifters also do speed training.)

All the characteristics of a muscle that contribute to the generation of force, i.e. all the strength factors such as fibre number, thickness etc., are important to speed. Quality of muscle in terms of *muscle fibre type* (see Chapter 3, page 93), is especially significant; individuals capable of explosive movements generally have a high percentage of so-called 'fast twitch' fibres in their muscles. Several body features, other than simply the characteristics of the muscles themselves, also contribute to speed. The most significant of these is *limb proportions*. As noted earlier, muscles act more effectively through short levers. However, although short limbs can therefore be moved faster, this advantage must be modified by considerations of the type of activity in which the speed is actually used; short legs provide stronger muscle action, but cover less ground per stride. Therefore, participants in different types of speed activity may all be able to generate great explosive force, but they are likely to differ in respect of the other components of speed; this is illustrated by the distinct body types of sprinters, high jumpers and weight lifters. Furthermore, these different types of speed activity involve their own particular patterns of movement, co-ordination and reaction. In other words, activities based on speed have a very high *skill component*.

Speed training. Many of the elements that contribute to speed are largely inherited, e.g. body proportions, muscle fibre type etc. In fact, the major trainable aspects of speed lie in the areas of speed skills, such as technique, style and reaction time.

Principles of speed training:
1. Speed training should be specific. The development of one aspect or type of speed does not necessarily have a beneficial

effect on other aspects (sprinting at top speed does not develop reaction time, or the ability to change direction or to stop or to start running). This means that speed training should consist of the actual types of movements required, rather than being aimed at the development of some general speed ability. And, as in skill training, a complete speed activity can be divided into sub-activities for their individual development.

2. Speed requires the development of other fitness components. That is, before speed can be fully expressed, other fitness components must be at fairly high levels; strength is required, to generate enough explosive force (the elastic component can be developed by, say, hopping or other forms of rebound movements); suppleness is important, since this determines the range of movement through which force can be applied; and muscular stamina is needed, to sustain speed for a useful length of time.

3. Speed training should not be restricted by limitations in other factors. Although speed is highly dependent on other components of fitness, the effectiveness of speed training is greatly lessened if attempts are made to train these components at the same time as speed. For example, running up steps is primarily a leg-strengthening exercise; the strength requirements of the activity quickly limit the extent of any benefits on actual speed. (Running down a gentle slope is a more effective method for developing leg speed.) Again, it must be clear whether repetition sprints are being used as a form of endurance training, or as a means of developing the speed skills involved in reaction time and direction changes; if it is the latter, then more recovery time must be allowed, otherwise requirements of stamina limit the speed that can be achieved.

Suppleness
The effect of this component on movement and posture can often give a bigger indication of an individual's general level of fitness (and age) than perhaps any other single factor. Suppleness contributes to fitness in two ways:

   i. it determines the range that the limbs can move through, and thus influences the extent to which other components of fitness can be expressed;

   ii. it is an important factor in injury avoidance, both sudden injury brought about by severe twists or distortions of the body, and longer term, chronic injury due to stressful, repetitive movement.

The suppleness of an individual is determined by the combined effects of two main features: *joint flexibility*, which determines the ultimate range of movement around the joint and which itself consists of the actual bone structure of the joint and the lengths of the connective ligaments that support the joint; and *muscle extensibility*, which is determined by the lengths of the muscles (and their tendons) that cross the joint.

It is widely believed that females are more supple than males, and children are markedly more supple than adults. However, it is not clear whether these differences are inevitable, or whether they result from differences in lifestyle and general activity. Certainly there is some loss of suppleness with age, as connective tissues, tendons and ligaments thicken, but due to the changes in types and levels of activity that also accompany aging, it is difficult to determine the real extent of actual aging effects.

Suppleness training. The different elements of suppleness show different levels of response to training. The extent of joint flexibility is largely inherited, although it can be increased to a certain degree particularly before adolescence. Extreme flexibility in certain joints is necessary for some sports (e.g. in the hips for hurdling and in the shoulders and ankles for efficient swimming), but in many sports the joints require as much support as possible. Therefore flexibility training aimed at changes in joint structure, or even at substantial change in ligament length, is likely to result in joint instability and a tendency towards injury.

Muscle extensibility, however, responds very markedly to training – and in two quite contrasting ways. Repeated contraction of a muscle results in a significant decrease in its resting length, and after a training session the exercised muscles can actually be shorter. Tight, inextensible muscles are a common characteristic of many sportsmen and women, and this is probably the basis for the misconception that exercise produces some kind of muscle-bound state. This condition can be readily corrected because the other way that a muscle responds to training is to increase markedly in length during specific stretching exercises. In fact, unusually for a component of fitness, improvement is often apparent after just a single training (stretching) session.

The general principles that govern suppleness training are outlined below; actual stretching exercises are described in the warm-up and cool-down routines given at the end of this chapter.

Principles of suppleness training:

1. Changes in suppleness are joint specific. That is, rather than being a general characteristic of the body, suppleness varies between different joints depending on the amounts and types of activity to which they are exposed. This applies both to the harmful shortening effects of repetitive exercise on a muscle, and to the beneficial effects of stretching exercises.

2. Stretching exercises should be carried out at the end of a training session. This provides an immediate counter to the muscle-shortening effects of training while the muscles are still warm; it is even more effective to have an additional stretching session about an hour later.

3. Stretching exercises should be carried out slowly and deliberately. It is counter-productive to use bouncing or jerky movements since these are likely to initiate the muscle 'stretch reflex' (the muscle protects itself against sudden stretching movements by reflexively contracting – see the section in Chapter 3, on how muscles work, page 95). The most effective method of stretching is to hold a stretch just at the point of discomfort for about 20 seconds, then reach for another half-inch. Dynamic, swinging movements are quite hazardous; uncontrollable momentum is being used and if an injury starts to occur during the swing, little can be done to stop it. And passive stretching, where an outside force is used to push a limb into extreme positions, is so potentially dangerous that it is to be positively discouraged – unless the outside force is a qualified individual.

Stamina

This is the capacity to repeat a movement or to continue an activity for some period of time. This ability to perform for longer, or with less effort, is the aspect of fitness that is probably of greatest general usefulness, and the development of stamina should thus occupy a major part of any training programme.

A general account of the physiological events that underlie 'stamina' is given in Chapter 3, in the section dealing with the provision of energy to the muscles, page 90. Briefly, processes within the muscle convert stored carbohydrate into the form of energy that powers muscle action, with oxygen playing a central role in these processes. Stamina is concerned with the total capacity of this energy provision system, and nowadays its various elements are referred to by different terms:

Cardiorespiratory fitness describes the capacity of the whole oxygen supply system; it includes processes of oxygen uptake into the body, which, of course, occur in the lungs, and for which it is not so much the actual size of the lungs that is important but rather the extent of the blood capillary network within them; and processes of oxygen transport around the body, in which the significant features are the total amount of blood available and the pumping capacity of the heart.

Local muscular endurance, on the other hand, describes the ability of a muscle to continue activity, and is based on features within the actual muscle itself. During activity of low-to-medium intensity, these local energy provision processes use the oxygen that is delivered by the cardiorespiratory system and are said to be functioning 'aerobically'; the capacity of the muscle to use this oxygen is determined by the levels of its own blood capillary network, energy-processing machinery and carbohydrate food store. (There is thus a close relationship, but not exact identity, between cardiorespiratory fitness and aerobic muscular endurance.) During high intensity activity, when enough oxygen cannot be supplied, additional energy provision processes operate within the muscle ('anaerobic' processes); the most significant feature of this anaerobic endurance system is its production of lactic acid.

Measurement of stamina. Since stamina is such a central component of fitness, its level is often used as a measure of general fitness. Several 'fitness tests' have been developed over the years to measure different aspects of stamina, e.g. in the 1940s the Harvard step-up test, in the 1960s the Cooper 12 minute run, and most recently the measurement of VO_2max. This last method involves measurement of the actual amount of oxygen used while the individual is working maximally at some physical task like running on a treadmill or pedalling a fixed bicycle. As a measure of the capacity of the body to

absorb, transport and utilise oxygen, the VO_2max is generally
accepted as the most useful indicator of aerobic power.

As far as the measurement of an individual's fitness is concerned, few of us have free access to a laboratory where
VO_2max can be determined; and the other tests are fairly
inaccurate. However, any measure of fitness is more meaning-
ful to the individual if it is related to improvement in his or
her own performance in some desired activity, rather than to
position in some Table of averaged fitness values. That is,
'getting fitter' simply means being able to do something better,
and this is true whether fitness is muscular endurance in the
arms as measured by press-ups, or the combination of leg
endurance and cardiorespiratory fitness that is measured by
running.

Stamina training. While there are many inherited limitations
on the absolute size of effort that can be exerted (i.e. on
strength), the time over which effort can be sustained can be
markedly increased. That is, stamina is highly responsive to
training, although different forms of training are required to
develop the different aspects of stamina.

Cardiorespiratory training. Virtually every aspect of the cardiorespiratory system changes in response to training; the
ability of the lungs to absorb oxygen is increased through a
greater development of their blood capillary network, the
total volume of blood in the body is increased by as much as
a litre, and the size and power of the heart are increased.
The greater pumping capacity of the heart is the basis of the
(generally) slower resting pulse rates of trained individuals –
the same amount of blood can be pumped by fewer beats –
but the massive difference between an 'untrained' and a
'trained' heart really becomes apparent when they are working
under load at their respective maximum capacities: the
untrained heart can pump about 14 litres of blood per minute
(around 120 beats per minute at about 120ml of blood per
beat), whereas a trained heart is likely to be capable of pumping over 30 litres per minute (190 bpm at 160ml per beat).

Principles of cardiorespiratory training:
*1. Training activities for cardiorespiratory fitness are non-
specific.* That is, the actual nature of the activity itself is unim-
portant as long as it stimulates the cardiorespiratory system;

any activity that raises the heart rate and maintains it at an appropriate training level for a long enough period, has a training effect on cardiorespiratory fitness. (In other words, the heart doesn't know, or care, whether it is activity of the arms or legs that is forcing it to work harder.)

2. Cardiorespiratory training requires an appropriate intensity. It is generally reckoned that the safe maximum heart rate for an individual is 220 minus the age (e.g. for a forty year-old, 180 beats per minute is the safe maximum); a good training effect can be obtained from a heart rate of 200 minus age; and the minimum rate for a significant training effect is around 180 minus age. Duration of activity is also important, and the heart rate should be maintained in its training range for at least 20 minutes.

3. Cardiorespiratory training is more effective if large muscle groups are used. Large muscle groups like those in the legs not only place greater demands on the cardiorespiratory system, but these are usually the only ones with enough local strength and endurance to be able to maintain activity for long enough to have a training effect on the system (e.g. most people cannot continue press-ups for long enough to receive any significant cardiorespiratory training effect). Therefore, activities like running and cycling are best for cardiorespiratory training.

Local endurance training. This aspect of stamina also shows a high response to training, and changes that occur within the muscle include further development of its blood capillary network and increases in its carbohydrate food stores and energy-processing machinery. However, there are some differences in training principles for local muscular endurance.

Principles of local endurance training:
1. Local endurance training must be specific. The local specificity of training effect on the muscles is seen in three respects: it is specific to the body part being exercised (exercising the arms has no effect on leg endurance); it is specific to the type of activity (cycling has little effect on the endurance of 'running muscles' even though both activities use the legs); and it is even fairly specific to the intensity of an activity (fast and slow-paced running place quite different demands on the aerobic capacity of a muscle).

2. Endurance training requires an appropriate intensity. This is where training effects on cardiorespiratory fitness and local aerobic endurance overlap. The optimum training intensity for the development of aerobic endurance is within the range of 75–90% of the maximum capacity; too low, and the aerobic system of the muscle is not stressed enough; too high, and the anaerobic system is brought into operation.

3. The duration of each endurance training session is important. The duration of each training exercise should be appropriate to the type of fitness that is required; just as six groups of 10 press-ups do not require the same muscular endurance as one group of 60 press-ups, so two runs of 5 miles each do not produce the endurance effect of a 10 mile run.

4. Anaerobic fitness requires specific training. The abilities to tolerate and detoxify the waste product, lactic acid, are not significantly developed by aerobic exercise. Anaerobic fitness training basically consists of creating a fairly substantial oxygen debt by, say, fast runs of 300 metres or so (shorter shuttle sprints generally allow too much recovery for the development of a significant anaerobic state).

However, anaerobic training should be treated cautiously – the body needs considerable time to remove lactic acid (sometimes longer than 24 hours). It is also arguable whether any specific anaerobic training at all is useful to a general fitness programme. The anaerobic system is inherently inefficient and can operate only for very limited periods (see Chapter 3, page 92). Therefore such training can produce extreme fatigue, without benefit to general fitness.

Skinniness

The term 'skinniness' is used to describe this component of fitness, instead of, say, 'slimness', in order to denote the specific absence of body fat rather than lack of weight or muscularity. And it is *fat* that is the real topic of this section.

Fat increases fitness for very few activities – in long distance swimming it is an advantage for increased insulation and buoyancy. In other sports, fat is a deadweight that must be carried around to no purpose; it provides no propulsive force, and it is not a significant source of energy for the short-term needs of sports activities (even in a 26 mile marathon, less than 0.25kg of fat is used). Therefore, one way of improving fitness in a single step consists simply of reducing body fat.

Because of differences in size and activity between individuals, it is not really possible to say exactly how much energy a body requires. However, unlike a petrol tank, the body does not overflow when too much energy is put into it. Excess energy is stored in two forms, carbohydrate and fat. The body's capacity to store carbohydrate is limited, but fat can be stored in virtually unlimited quantities, and excess carbohydrate is converted to fat. Weight for weight, fat contains over twice the energy of carbohydrate, but it acts as an energy store only for some biological crisis. That is, fat is not readily available for use and the body must be placed under considerable stress before fat-stored energy is called upon; even body protein may be used as a source of energy before the fat stores are depleted to any significant extent (a disadvantage in trying to lose weight simply by dieting).

One of the reasons why body fat is not available as an energy source is that, whereas carbohydrate is stored within the working muscles themselves, fat is largely stored in other locations in specially developed *fat storage cells* (note that there is no connection or interconversion between muscle cells and fat-storing cells). The distribution of these 'fat' cells throughout the body is not random, and, unfortunately, is not controllable. Fat storage areas are specifically distributed according to features of sex, age and genetic inheritance; males accumulate fat on the front of the body (chest and lower abdomen), females on the rear (lower torso and thighs); more fat storage cells usually develop with age, as the body's energy needs decline faster than energy intake; and an individual's own genetic inheritance determines the particular features of his or her fat distribution.

Measurement of body fat. In the first place, bodyweight alone does not necessarily give an accurate indication of an individual's level of body fat, since weight includes such additional features as muscle, bones etc. Nor is bodyweight a good means of monitoring the progress of an exercise programme since many of these features develop further with training, and muscle is more dense than fat (weight can actually increase with exercise, although fat is lost and body shape changes for the better). It is generally accepted that skinfold measurement, or *the pinch test*, gives a fairly accurate estimate of body fat. This simply involves measuring the thickness of the subcutaneous fat in pinched skinfolds at various parts of the body (e.g. upper arm, above the hip, under the shoulder blade) and then determining from a Table the percentage body fat that these measurements represent. However, it is even simpler to stand naked in front of a mirror, tense all the muscles and jump up and down; any skin that wobbles, is fat!

Body fat levels do vary widely between different types of people. For example, an average, untrained male may have as much as 18% body fat (this means a 160 lb individual is carrying around about 28 lb of fat); the level in a similar sort of female may be about 24% body fat; a reasonably fit, trained individual may be around 12%; a distance runner would be likely to be around 8% due to the energy requirements and stress of training, but bodybuilders have been recorded as having less than 5% body fat, this being achieved through the combined effects of training and the strict control of fat in the diet. (Female bodybuilders have also come close to these levels, which tends to argue against the notion that females 'must' carry a layer of subcutaneous fat.)

Training for fat loss. Skinniness is a highly trainable component of fitness. However, only the size of fat storage cells is reversible by training and diet (control of their number or distribution requires the surgeon's scalpel). Restriction of food intake is one obvious way of controlling body fat, particularly restriction of the amount of fat itself that is eaten, and in some sports a special diet is an integral part of training (bodybuilding). But attempts to reduce body fat *solely* by dieting are counter-productive in several respects: a special diet involves abnormal eating habits whose benefits are lost when the normal eating pattern is re-established; in the absence of exercise, dieting may result in the loss of body protein rather than fat; and the more severe the diet, the more the rate of body metabolism actually slows down, resulting in a greater tendency to put on fat when the diet is stopped. These difficulties disappear if an exercise programme is carried out along with the diet, and exercise itself has additional advantages as a means of losing fat: regular exercise brings about a higher rate of energy utilisation even when the body is at rest, i.e. there is a carry over effect from exercise; it can act as an appetite suppressant, through its effects on blood sugar levels; and it affects body shape by developing muscle tone.

The amounts of energy used in different activities and the

energy budget of exercise in general are described in Chapter 3, in the section on food and fitness (page 98). However, the general principles, that should guide any exercise programme aimed primarily at fat reduction, are outlined here.

Principles of training for fat loss:

1. Extent of energy use should not be equated with intensity of effort. The amount of energy used up in an activity is more or less the energy that is required simply to move a certain mass a certain distance. Considerations of intensity of effort involve other factors, such as the actual strength and endurance of the muscle groups in relation to the task they have to perform. Thus a very intense or difficult activity may involve relatively little energy use. For example, 50 press-ups may require a great deal of effort, but they only require the energy to move 150 lb through 50 yards (bodyweight and arm length, 50 times); on the other hand, the easy activity of a 10 minute walk at 3 mph uses over 10 times this amount of energy (150 lb moved through 880 yards). Therefore, puffing and sweating is not necessarily the best way to burn off the calories.

2. Duration of activity is more important than intensity of effort. The reason for this is that a very great increase in effort does not require a *correspondingly* great increase in energy utilisation. For example, jogging at a pace of 9 minutes per mile uses energy at about 14.5 Kcals per minute (130.5 Kcals per mile); running at 7 minutes per mile uses about 19 Kcals per minute (133 Kcals per mile). That is, running at a pace that is felt to be *much* faster, only uses about an extra 3 Kcals per mile. Alternatively, if the slower pace is jogged at for an extra 5 minutes, then another 72.5 Kcals are used. Therefore, for purposes of energy utilisation, it is better to exercise at a moderate intensity for a longer period than at high intensity for a short period. (Note that 1 nutritional calorie is 1000 heat calories, or 1 Kcal, see page 97.)

3. Many short training sessions are as effective as fewer long sessions. Although duration of activity is important for fat reduction, approximately the same amount of energy is required for an hour's exercise of a particular type at a particular intensity, whether the activity occurs in one session or in many short sessions; one hour's jogging at 9 minutes per mile uses 870 Kcals whether it takes place in 60 minutes or in 6 sessions of 10 minutes. Therefore, for fat reduction it is the *total* duration of activity that is important, in a day, in a week, and in a month; regularity of activity is the key factor.

There is therefore quite a difference in approach between training for 'fitness' and training for fat reduction; fitness requires intensity (for cardiorespiratory effect) and duration (for endurance purposes); fat reduction requires simply the most efficient method of burning energy. This means that an individual who is primarily interested in fat reduction perhaps should not, and certainly need not, suffer intense fitness-type training in the initial stages of an exercise programme.

Misconceptions about fat, diet and exercise:

1. *Muscles turn into fat*. No. These cell types are quite separate. This fallacy probably arises from the observation that many ex-sportsmen are overweight, a situation that is simply due to the imbalance between food intake and energy expenditure; the eating habits of the sporting career are continued into retirement.

2. *Fat can be lost in different ways*. No. Fat cannot be dissolved, steamed, massaged, pummelled, vibrated or electrocuted away. The fat stores may be physically broken up to a small extent, but the only way for fat to be actually removed is by being used as an energy source – or by being cut off.

3. *Fat can be lost from chosen areas.* No. The distribution of fat storage areas is determined by genetic background, sex and age; and the utilisation of fat is determined by the general metabolism of the body. Exercise of a particular muscle does not necessarily use fat from the storage area nearest to it. (But exercise may affect the appearance of certain body parts through effects on muscle tone.)

4. *Dieting is the best way to lose fat*. No. Weight can be lost, but this usually is not due wholly to fat loss. In addition, the effects of dieting on the body's metabolism often lead to an even greater tendency to gain fat when the diet is stopped.

5. *Exercise makes you gain weight because you eat more*. Not necessarily. Weight may increase slightly, but this is not due to increased fat. It is more likely to be due to increased fitness and muscle tone. Also, if carried out regularly, exercise need not result in an increased appetite.

Sports activities and fitness

In this section, the effects of the more common types of sports activities on the different components of fitness are summarised, along with comments on their advantages and limitations for the development of fitness in general. (In most cases, of course, these effects of sport on particular aspects of fitness simply mirror the requirements of that sport for particular aspects of fitness; but note that this relationship does not exactly hold for 'games fitness'.)

Running – This activity-cum-sport obviously develops endurance and strength in the legs; other effects depend on the actual type of running.

Fitness factors – Jogging, with no rise in heart rate, puts little or no stress on the cardiorespiratory system, and is mainly useful only for the control of body fat. However, since it is full bodyweight that is being continuously moved around, some form of walking, jogging or running is the most effective way of burning off calories. Running so that the heart rate is raised to its appropriate training level (180–200 minus age) for 20–40 minutes, develops cardiorespiratory fitness and aerobic endurance. Severe breathlessness induces an anaerobic condition, which has little significance for general fitness.

Comments – Running is a simple, convenient activity with strong positive effects on several important fitness factors. Its limitations are that it has no effects on upper body fitness, and, less obviously, its highly repetitive movements can result in a great loss in suppleness, and in the development of imbalance between particular muscle groups.

Cycling – Although cycling, like running, involves leg movement, quite different muscle groups are used, and therefore trained, in the two activities.

Fitness factors – Cycling develops cardiorespiratory fitness, if the work rate is high enough, and specific leg endurance. Its repetitive movements lead to a loss of suppleness.

Comments – Cycling is a very efficient means of locomotion, the body does not have to be supported against gravity, and (relatively) little stress is placed on the joints. This means that the body can tolerate training loads that develop exceptional endurance and cardiorespiratory capacities (heart rates in excess of 200 bpm have been recorded in racing cyclists during a sprint finish – at the end of 100 miles of racing). It also means that in cycling a more deliberate effort has to be made to raise the heart rate into an effective training range (stately commuting by bicycle does little for fitness), and that greater distances have to be covered in training (it is generally reckoned that around 4 miles of cycling is equivalent to 1 mile of running).

Canoeing – Consideration of this activity also serves to illustrate an important point about fitness training, particularly cardiorespiratory training.
Fitness factors – Local endurance is developed in specific muscles of the torso, shoulders and arms.
Comments – Although the work intensity in canoeing is very high, and consequently needs a high aerobic capacity, it uses muscles that are smaller and relatively weaker than the large muscles of the hips and legs. In terms of general fitness training, few individuals, except competitive canoeists themselves, have the upper body strength and stamina to sustain an adequate canoeing rate for a long enough period to receive any cardiorespiratory benefit.

Swimming – There are several good reasons for including this activity in a fitness programme, although it also has some limitations.
Fitness factors – Swimming exercises all the major muscles of both the upper and lower body. The stretching and pulling movements are particularly useful for maintaining suppleness. The heart can increase in size by about 15% while the body is submerged and horizontal (i.e. it has a greater capacity for harder work), which means that swimming can have very great effects on the cardiorespiratory system – if the training intensity is appropriate (see below).
Comments – The 'non-stressful' nature of swimming, in terms of the support the body receives from the water and the lack of jarring or pounding effects, has several consequences. It means that swimming can be a useful form of exercise during injury or at the beginning of a training programme. It also means that phenomenal training loads can be tolerated (the training load of a club swimmer is reckoned to be equivalent to 200 miles a week by a runner). This, plus the effects of swimming on the heart, probably accounts for the extremely high cardiorespiratory capacities of swimmers. But the rate

of energy utilisation in swimming is relatively low (just over half that of jogging, see Chapter 3, page 98). Therefore recreational swimming is not a very effective means of weight reduction. Furthermore, many people just cannot swim well enough to maintain their heart rates at an adequate training level for a sufficient length of time (they would probably obtain a better training effect simply by using a floatboard and a steady leg pumping action).

Gymnastics and Martial Arts – These activities are grouped together because of the similarities of their requirements for, and effects upon, fitness.

Fitness factors – Besides the particular aspects of skill unique to each, all of these activities develop extremely high levels of strength, speed, stamina and suppleness throughout the body. They probably come closest to the actual realisation of any notion of total physical fitness.

Comments – In gymnastics, the relatively short nature of individual events in competition means that there is less emphasis on cardiorespiratory fitness; in the martial arts, the periods of activity are considerably longer and require much higher aerobic capacities.

Keep-fit and Aerobics Classes – These activities, of course, are specially designed to improve general fitness, but they have some limitations.

Fitness factors – A well-constructed fitness session contains various elements: an appropriate warm-up (see the section on Training, at the end of this chapter, page 39); fairly intense activity that keeps the heart rate continuously high for 20 minutes or so and develops cardiorespiratory fitness; exercises to develop the local strength and endurance of other major muscle groups in the upper and lower body; and a serious stretching session to develop suppleness.

Comments – These activities do offer ways of improving most aspects of general fitness, although their effectiveness can be greatly lessened by the circumstances under which they are carried out. In large classes there is sometimes a lack of instruction, which can result in inadequate or faulty technique, or even in injury (particularly in aerobics classes the instructor often seems to be more concerned with leading and demonstrating, than with teaching). Again, in a generalised programme for a large class, the training intensity may not be appropriate to the individual's level of fitness, either too difficult (with loss of continuity of effort) or too easy (with insufficient stress for a training effect). And another point that applies particularly to aerobics classes, is that there is often no training progression built into the programme, an aspect that is essential to any fitness development.

Games fitness – Only the general nature of the relationship between games and fitness is considered here; training recommendations for particular games are given in Chapter 2.

Fitness factors – The actual skills of a particular game are developed by direct game practice (and only by game practice – see section on 'skill', page 12). Games are somewhat unusual, however, in that other components of fitness that are required for the game, are not necessarily developed by playing the game. This applies to strength and suppleness, but is particularly true for certain aspects of stamina.

Comments – Most physical games, whether team games like football and hockey, or individual games like squash and tennis, all consist of periods of anaerobic effort overlaid on a background of aerobic activity (see Chapter 3, page 91, for a full explanation of these terms). It is now well-established that, although the positive (scoring) movements of a game may involve anaerobic activity, there is a direct relationship between the standard of play and the level of aerobic activity: the higher the standard of play, the greater the aerobic fitness of the players. The reason that high aerobic fitness is so useful, is simply that it allows a greater proportion of the game to be played in an aerobic condition, rather than in an inefficient, fatiguing anaerobic state. This results in less tiredness during the game, and quicker recovery between games. Now, the anaerobic aspect of fitness may be developed by actually playing the game, but there are several reasons why aerobic fitness is not greatly affected by the game itself. Firstly, anaerobic activity does not develop aerobic fitness; secondly, the levels of activity in the aerobic phases of the game are unlikely to be intense or continuous enough to maintain a high aerobic training condition; and thirdly, a combination of increasing skill and experience, and dependence on colleagues in team sports, can substitute for fitness (an older sportsman who depends, say, on a game like squash to 'keep fit', can maintain performance through increasing guile, while fitness actually declines). Aerobic fitness for games is most effectively developed by steady running (see Chapter 2); any serious games player should be able at least to run 3 miles in 18–20 minutes – many of the All Blacks rugby players are actually 'marathon trained' before the start of the rugby season!

Therefore, a game can provide a high level of motivation for attaining fitness, but for various reasons does not itself provide the best physical training for achieving fitness. The situation is summed up in the old adage that *a player should get fit for the game, not use the game to get fit.*

What Is Training?

The word 'training' has been used quite often so far, and it is appropriate at this point to consider exactly what it means. A 'training effect' involves an actual change in some feature of the body, that results in an improved performance in some activity or other. For this change to occur, the body must be provided with an activity (a stimulus) that forces it to change; if the activity can be handled comfortably with no effort or stress, then there is no reason for the body to change or improve. This aspect of stress-induced change distinguishes training from simple exercise or recreational activity, and is the key feature that most of the general principles of training are based around.

General training principles:

1. The training stress should be appropriate for the type of fitness that is required. Training is specific. This has already been pointed out in relation to the specificity of training effects in skill, strength and muscular endurance; except for the generalised effects on the cardiorespiratory system, the effects of training are more or less restricted to the parts of the body that are actually exercised, and specific for the types and intensities of movements that are carried out. This specificity of effect is the main reason for being quite clear about the reasons for training, whether it be simply to lose weight or to develop particular components of fitness for a sport.

2. The training stress should be progressive. As the body adapts to the training stress imposed on it, and improves, then obviously the original training level is no longer going to be stressful enough to act as a physiological stimulus. The nature of the progression is determined by the overall aims and objectives of training, but in general, greater fitness should involve 'better' training rather than simply 'more' training; that is, as fitness improves, training sessions should become faster or more intense or involve heavier loads, rather than simply becoming longer.

3. Rest is as important as stress. The body obviously requires time to recover from the training stress that is imposed on it. Such recovery periods can take two forms – periods of inactivity (passive rest) or periods of light exercise, stretching or massage (active rest). Active rest seems generally to result in faster recovery, through effects of the circulatory system on waste product removal and nutrient replenishment. However, another point to realise about this aspect of training is that this is also the period in which the physiological adaptations to training actually take place; that is, the training effect occurs after, not during, a training session. (At first glance this may seem surprising, but obviously nothing actually improves during a fitness session since performance is poorer at the end of it than it was at the start.)

4. Training is a controlled balance of stress and recovery. The complete training process thus consists of two equally necessary aspects: stressful activity depletes energy stores, produces waste products and generally breaks down the body; during recovery, energy stores are replenished, waste products removed and the body built up again. If the balances within and between these two aspects are correct, recovery actually 'overshoots' to a higher level – a training effect occurs. The sequences of breakdown and recovery that result from different training situations are shown in the accompanying diagrams (Fig. 2): obviously, stress that is not intense enough or frequent enough does not improve fitness, but conversely, too much stress, or too little rest, can actually damage fitness.

5. It is possible to overtrain. Performance can deteriorate if recovery is not complete between training sessions (see line c in the diagram). Such overtraining can occur at all levels of fitness, and even before deterioration in actual performance, there are other signs that a training regime may be too stressful. These are listed below. Oddly enough, the greatest likelihood of overtraining does not arise from individually hard sessions, when it is clear that the body has been treated harshly and

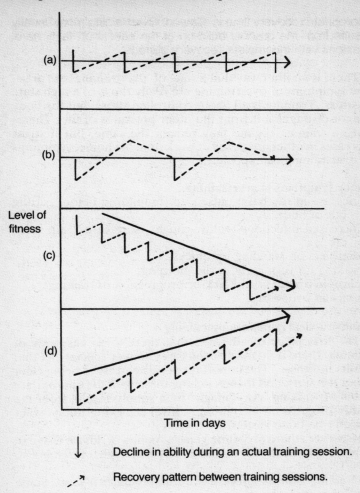

Level of
fitness

Time in days

↓   Decline in ability during an actual training session.

⌐⌐↗   Recovery pattern between training sessions.

Fig. 2 Effects of various sequences of training and recovery on level of fitness.
   (a) Not much training stress, no improvement in fitness.
   (b) Adequate training stress, infrequent sessions, no improvement in fitness.
   (c) Adequate training stress, inadequate recovery, deterioration in fitness.
   (d) Balance of stress and recovery, steady improvement in fitness.

appropriate recovery time is allowed. Overtraining more usually results from the gradual build-up of the effects of 'fairly hard' sessions with incomplete recovery periods.

There is another way that a state of 'overtraining' can arise. The symptoms of overtraining are really those of a high state of stress. Training is all about controlled stress, but the body cannot distinguish it from the other pressures of life. There-fore, a training regime may remain the same, but if stress increases in other areas, say at work or in the home, symptoms of overtraining can appear.

Major symptoms of overtraining:
   increase in the basal pulse rate (monitored before getting out of bed);
   increased infections (colds, coughs, sore throat, lip sores etc.);
   dizziness on standing up quickly;
   waking up very early in the morning;
   chronic tiredness and lack of progression in training;
   unusual irritability.

Some practical points about training
   The first piece of advice is that there is no easy way of training; there is no magic exercise system or special diet that results in fitness. The important points consist of being clear about the aims, and then matching these with the appropriate forms of training. Any 'magic' then simply results from the steady progression in training – from achieving today, what couldn't be done yesterday.
   However, there are some general points of advice that can increase the effectiveness, and safety, of all types of training.

1. Training is more effective if a training diary is used. Some kind of record of each training session is probably the most useful single training aid at all levels of performance. It gives encouragement by providing evidence of progress – or acts as a spur by indicating the lack of it. Its record of forgotten falls, twists or changes in training pattern can also be useful in tracing the causes of injuries, particularly the kind that appear for 'no reason'. The actual details in the diary depend, of course, on the type of training but could include:
   conditions – date, time, weather, terrain (if appropriate);

performance – miles, times, exercise details (weight, repetitions etc.);
happenings – incidents, accidents, injuries;
comments – feeling tired, good, sore etc.

All this information can be quickly recorded in an appropriate
type of chart or log-book.

2. The beginnings and ends of training sessions are important.
Warm-up and cool-down routines not only increase the effectiveness of training, but also help to counter the harmful
effects of training (injury and loss of suppleness). Actual exercises and routines are suggested at the end of this section.

Warm-up: This has several purposes, whose emphases vary
according to the intended activity. Before a training session
the aims are simply:

   i.   to stretch the muscles gradually, rather than in sud-
       den training (and tearing) movements;
  ii.   to warm and mobilise the muscles, and get the circu-
       lation going.

These two aims are best achieved by carrying out some
gentle stretching, then some movement, then stretching over
a greater range, then more dynamic movements, and so on
for about 5–10 minutes. Before a competitive event, a warm-
up includes additional aims:

 iii.   to raise the pulse rate to the appropriate level for
       the event;
 iv.   to provide the psychological preparation for the event
       (and this may be the most important aspect of all).

The extent of the warm-up can vary with the conditions and
the nature of the activity: if the weather is warm, the body
needs little warming by physical activity; and while a sprinter
needs extensive pre-event preparation, there is no physical
need to spend 30 minutes warming-up for a marathon.

(Various types of liniments and sporting rubs are often
applied during the warm-up. These generally consist of some
mixture of an analgesic, or pain-relieving substance, and a
vasodilatant, which increases local blood circulation and thus
reddens the skin. Most authorities would deny that these
substances have any real practical benefit – yet most users
would not be without them. Certainly they have effects on

local circulation and heating, and the rubbing required for their application is also beneficial. Nor can it do any harm to feel that at least you 'smell fit'.)

Cool-down: This should cover two aspects:

i. a gradual lessening of activity over a period of a few minutes, rather than a sudden halt, helps to get the circulation started on the removal of waste products;

ii. a serious stretching session helps to prevent painful muscle stiffness in the short term, and loss of suppleness in the long term.

The stretching session should consist of at least 10 minutes of deliberate and intense stretching, following the principles discussed in the section on suppleness: bouncing, jerky movements should be avoided; the most effective method is to stretch to the point of discomfort, hold that position for 20–30 seconds, then reach further.

Warm-up and cool-down routines: Although a routine must be thorough, the simpler it is, the more likely it is to be carried out; it is also useful to develop a set pattern for going through the movements, for example starting at one end of the body and working towards the other.

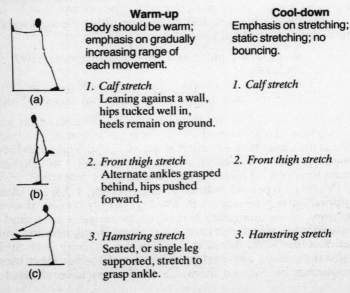

	Warm-up	**Cool-down**
	Body should be warm; emphasis on gradually increasing range of each movement.	Emphasis on stretching; static stretching; no bouncing.
(a)	*1. Calf stretch* Leaning against a wall, hips tucked well in, heels remain on ground.	*1. Calf stretch*
(b)	*2. Front thigh stretch* Alternate ankles grasped behind, hips pushed forward.	*2. Front thigh stretch*
(c)	*3. Hamstring stretch* Seated, or single leg supported, stretch to grasp ankle.	*3. Hamstring stretch*

(d)

4. *Back, hips, ankle stretch* Deep knee bend, *heels on ground,* arms out in front for balance.

4. *Back, hips, ankle stretch*

(e)

5. *Groin stretch* Front lunge position, both feet face forwards.

5. *Groin stretch*

(f)

6. *Groin stretch* Sideways lunge position.

6. *Groin stretch*

(g)

7. *Arm circling* Large circles, arms brush ears.

7. *Bar hanging* Simply hanging from a bar for 30–60 seconds, stretches the shoulders, back and hips.

(h)

8. *Side bends* No forward lean, no bouncing.

(i)

9. *Trunk twisting* Wide leg position, hips remain facing forwards.

Common mistakes in training

Much physical activity that is performed under the name of 'training' is fairly ineffective (or even downright harmful).

Some of the more commonly committed (and omitted) errors
are listed below. The aspects that relate particularly to running, circuit training and weight training are discussed more
fully in the appropriate sections of Chapter 2.

Aimless training
e.g. overall purpose not clear;
      short-term objectives not clear;
      no stress or effort in training;
      no progression in training;
      no training diary or record of progress.

Inappropriate training
(training methods do not match training aims)
e.g. intense bursts of activity, aiming for weight loss;
      dozens of press-ups, aiming for strength gains;
      ineffective level of heart rate in circuit training;
      ineffective running pace for aerobic development; .
      running greater and greater distances, in order to achieve
          a faster marathon time.

Overtraining
e.g. no illness, but performance deteriorates;
      training intensified, performance deteriorates.

Inappropriate stretching
e.g. not stretching at all;
      not stretching after training;
      stretching under poor conditions (cold);
      stretching with poor technique (bouncing, swinging);
      high leg kicks before stretching or warming-up.

Poor exercise technique (especially in weight training)
e.g. short, jerky, bouncing movements;
      no full range of movement in an exercise;
      uncontrolled swinging movements using momentum;
      no effort in the positive (raising) movement;
      no control in the negative (lowering) movement.

2

KEY TRAINING ACTIVITIES

This chapter describes the three key activities of running, circuit training and weight training. Different sports may place particular emphasis on one or other of these, but each of them is usually required to some degree – and all of them must certainly be carried out for general fitness training.

Running

This is the central component of any fitness programme, and is the single activity that provides the greatest benefits to overall fitness through its effects on heart-lung performance, endurance and bodyweight. However, different types of running, in terms of intensity and duration, develop different aspects of fitness to different extents.

Types of running

Slow and fast running should be thought of as terms which are related to the fitness and ability of the individual, rather than as particular speeds; what is slow for one person can be extremely fast for another. Training intensity can be judged by pulse rate (low intensity – pulse rate little changed from basal rate; high intensity – pulse rate = 200 minus individual's age). But it is inconvenient to keep track of pulse rate during a run and a rough guide can be obtained by estimating intensity as a percentage of maximum effort. For example, suppose 300 metres can be run in 60 seconds, 10% of this time is 6 seconds, therefore 300 metres at 90% effort would take 66 seconds; again, if a mile can be run in the fastest time of 6 minutes, a pace of 80% effort would be around 7 minutes 12 seconds per mile (6 minutes + 2 × 36 seconds). This method, though, is more unreliable, the greater the distance involved.

Jogging

Description – This is a pace that is well within the capacity of the individual, and could be anything from less than 7 minutes to more than 10 minutes per mile. The point is that it involves no effort and causes little rise in pulse rate.

Effects – Such activity obviously provides only low cardiorespiratory training, but it develops or maintains some leg endurance and, more significantly, it helps to control bodyweight.

Comments – Transport of the full weight of the body upon its own legs is the most effective means of using up calories. Some form of walking-jogging is therefore the best way of adjusting or controlling bodyweight, both for a beginner in the initial stages of a fitness programme and for a more experienced individual during a period of injury that prevents full training.

Aerobic endurance running

Description – This consists of sustained, even-paced running that imposes some degree of stress without, however, developing a significant state of breathlessness. Within this general category, different intensities of effort give slightly different training effects and are thus used for different purposes.

Effects – At *low intensities*, around 70% effort, the pace is easily sustained and results in only a slightly raised pulse rate. However, it is distinguished from jogging by the presence of some degree of training stress, this stress arising from the distance covered rather than from the pace. Therefore this type of running still has a relatively low cardiorespiratory training effect, and stronger effects on muscular endurance. *Fast-paced aerobic running* involves working at over 80% effort, with the pulse rate well up into the cardiorespiratory training range. It is sustained for periods of 20–60 minutes and thus also has strong effects on muscular endurance.

Comments – Low intensity running is used to develop the ability to handle distance, and is therefore carried out not only by beginners but also by more experienced runners preparing, say, for a marathon (albeit at different 'low intensity' paces, and at different distances from perhaps 3–20 miles).

Fast-paced aerobic running is the basic conditioning activity for virtually all aspects of physical fitness. It is also central to the aerobic fitness that is necessary for most games players (see page 34), and the early stages of their basic training programmes should include runs of 20–30 minutes *at this sort of pace*. (All serious games players, in whatever position, should be able at least to run 3 miles in 18–20 minutes – and very serious players, 5 miles in 30 minutes.)

Interval running

Description – This consists of repeated intervals of intense running, alternating with timed recovery periods. The critical features are: the length of the running interval remains the same throughout the training session; the intense pace of around 90% effort is sustained over each interval; the rests are strictly timed and remain the same length throughout the session; recovery is not complete between each interval.

Effects – Different lengths of running interval give different types of major training effect. *Short intervals* consist of runs of 15 seconds – 4 minutes duration; within this category, the shorter intervals can be accomplished almost wholly anaerobically, but runs lasting a minute or more require increasing cardiorespiratory input; a commonly used interval is around 300 metres at 90% effort, a single training session consisting of 10–20 such repetitions with a timed minute's rest between each. *Long intervals* of 4–15 minutes require a much higher aerobic input and have a very strong cardiorespiratory effect; however the difficulty of sustaining near maximum pace for these lengths of time restricts their use to serious distance runners. *Hill intervals* are carried out on long, not too steep slopes that allow 2–4 minutes of intense but positive running (no slowing); this type combines the requirements for great leg strength, high cardiorespiratory fitness and deep anaerobic capacity.

Comments – Interval running is a very strenuous form of endurance training that is aimed at developing the capability for sustaining effort.

Training progression is carried out by extending the period of effort, rather than by raising the level of pace. That is, the number of intervals in a session is increased, or the length of the rest periods is shortened.

Repetition running

Description – This also consists of fast-paced runs over set distances, but full recovery is allowed between each repetition.

Effects – The lengths of the repetitions are determined by the training aims. Short repetitions of 2–5 minutes make up the speed training for distance running. Long repetitions act as time trials for the actual type of event.

Comments – This type of running is aimed at increasing the pace itself, and is carried out mainly by the serious competitive runner.

Fartlek running

Description – The word fartlek is Swedish for 'speedplay' and it consists of a mixture of different types of running within a single session, constructed according to personal mood and the nature of the terrain – sprints up certain slopes, steady jogs to particular landmarks, fast-paced runs for different distances etc.

Effects – This variety develops all aspects of running fitness in a much less stressful way than the formal interval and repetition methods, and regular fartlek sessions are very useful to a general fitness training programme.

Comments – This form of training is also useful for groups of mixed abilities, by allowing handicapped bursts of running over different parts of a route or round loops of different lengths.

Games sprints

Besides basic fast-paced aerobic running, various types of sprints can be useful for developing speed for games players.

Flat sprints should be carried out over distances of 40–50 metres – full speed is usually reached by this point, and running further than this begins to rely more heavily on endurance rather than speed.

Downhill sprints along a gentle decline minimise running resistance and allow the 'free-wheeling' development of leg speed.

Uphill sprints develop leg strength and endurance; the steeper the gradient, the greater the strength requirement; the longer the gradient, the greater the endurance element.

Shuttle runs with their stops, starts, and changes of direction develop leg strength, acceleration, agility and balance for various game situations.

Walk sprints are a useful form of 'in-season' training for reaction time and acceleration. They can be done with a group reacting to general commands but are more effectively done in pairs. The pair walk, one a few paces behind the other; this rear partner chooses when to say 'go', and at the same time attempts to overtake the now-sprinting front partner *within five or six strides*. After a few repetitions the rôles are reversed.

Progression in running

In running, as in all forms of training, there must be progression, and over a period of time, a running programme should progress through several different stages, each of which has its own distinct aims and methods. These are indicated below, together with some ideas on the levels of performance that should be aimed at, before it is really worthwhile progressing on to the next stage.

Stages in running development:

1. Preliminary preparations. Before starting running, it may be necessary both to adjust bodyweight and to become used to activity. In cycling and swimming the joints are not subjected to such weight stress, but some form of walking/jogging is the most effective way to use up calories. The aims in this preliminary phase are simply to be less than 25 lb overweight, and to be able to sustain 30 minutes of continuous locomotion.

2. Training for distance (duration). The primary aims at the start of an actual running programme are to increase the distance or duration of the run. Running should consist of the low intensity aerobic type, with endurance and aerobic capacity being built up through the mild stress of increasing distance. Running can be carried out every day, but the total mileage (total running time) for the week should not increase by more than 20% in any one week. Whether training for general fitness, games or a marathon, this phase of low intensity running should last until about an hour's steady activity can be maintained (say, 6–8 miles). At this point it may be more appropriate to increase the training load by increasing the pace rather than continuing to increase the distance.

3. Training for pace. When an increased pace is being established, the distance should be shortened, perhaps by as much as 30–40%. It is productive in this phase to vary the pace within a run, for example by fartlek running. Another means of developing sustained pace is the so-called out and back method: this simply involves running 'out' over a fairly flat route for a noted time, then turning round and running back, trying to beat the outward time. By this stage, fairly fast-paced aerobic running should have become established (5 miles in 35 minutes; 3 miles in 18 minutes).

4. Continued progression. This requires appropriate juggling of pace and distance in programmes that include all the previously described types of running; the general rule is first to develop the pace, then apply this pace to increasing distance. However, although both pace and distance are manipulated for progression, it is important to realise that they really represent separate elements of running fitness. Running *far* does not directly increase the ability to run fast; training at 8 minutes per mile is unlikely to result in a 3 hour marathon time, no matter how many miles are covered in a week. Running *fast* does not necessarily develop the capacity to cover long distances; in terms of the training effect on local muscular endurance, two 5 mile runs are not equivalent to one 10 mile run.

5. Join a club. By this stage, the running programme has gone beyond simple fitness training and the advice and coaching of a running club are required.

Running style

This is a very personal characteristic; a running acquaintance can usually be recognised even though he or she is only a blur in the distance or a silhouette. Such aspects of running style need not, and probably cannot, be changed, but there are certain points that can make running both more effective and more enjoyable.

Some comments on running style:

1. Relax. This applies particularly to the upper body. The shoulders should remain relaxed and not twist or rotate with each stride, a habit caused by moving the arms across the front of the body with the elbows at a fixed angle. It also helps to think consciously from time to time of relaxing the arms and unclenching the fists.

2. Don't overstride. One sign of overstriding is that the horizon moves up and down (indicating that it is you who is bouncing up and down). Another is that the heel strikes the ground first, followed by the rest of the foot slapping the ground. The advantages of correcting stride length are as much for efficiency as for comfort. If the leading foot lands in front of the body in distance running, it actually tends to check forward momentum rather like the effects of leaning backwards when running downhill. The leading foot should land fairly flat directly under the hips, and the legs should propel the body like wheels rather than like flapping flails.

3. Invest in a good pair of running shoes. As the only things between the soft body and hard ground, shoes are the most important item of a runner's equipment. They not only cushion the feet but also help to protect the ankles, knees, hips and back against the constant jarring and pounding. The best place to buy shoes is in a shop staffed by runners, who can advise on the most suitable shoes for the individual's build and type of running; they can also suggest the best shoes to compensate for any peculiarities of running style such as pronation or supination. (Basically, pronators turn the foot outwards and land on the inside edge of the foot, supinators roll the foot inwards and land on the outside edge; the extremes of both styles can cause problems in the knees and hips.)

4. Look up, not down at your feet. That is, keep the head up, looking forwards with the shoulders relaxed, rather than shuffling along with the shoulders hunched and the head hanging down. (Difficult at the end of a marathon perhaps, but worth it in terms of breathing and self-esteem.)

Finally, it's a general truth that the runner who gets furthest, in racing and in training, is the one who remains relaxed and who retains style, not the one who drives and pushes. Running for fitness should also be approached in this manner, as a continuing activity which *gradually* produces positive body changes, not as a barrier or challenge that must be smashed through. Therefore, float and glide, rather than punch and drive – but cherish your hills as a test of fitness!

Circuit Training

This form of training develops stamina. It consists of a series, or circuit, of exercises for different parts of the body, that are worked through in a particular sequence. However, the same sequence of exercises can be carried out in two quite different ways, which put slightly different emphases on different aspects of stamina: 'circuit training', in the strict sense of the term, has a strong effect on cardiorespiratory fitness; 'stage training', in which each exercise is completed as a separate stage, puts more emphasis on muscular endurance.

Circuit training

In the form in which it was originally developed in the 1950s, circuit training involves about 10 or so different exercises arranged in a sequence so that different parts of the body are worked alternately. The individual is first tested on each exercise to determine his or her personal training level, in terms of numbers of repetitions to be performed. A 20–30 minute training session then consists of working continuously through the circuit, partially recovering between circuits and completing 3–5 circuits in the session. The whole point of this method is that the circuit is continuous, and the alternating sequence of the exercises, together with the tested personal training level, mean that a high work rate, and thus high heart rate, can be maintained. Therefore, the actual exercises have some effects on local muscular endurance, but the continuity of activity means that great training pressure is placed on the cardiorespiratory system.

Technique of circuit training:

1. Circuit construction. A circuit simply consists of 9–12 exercises that alternately work different body parts, and that maintain a high heart rate and oxygen consumption. Two examples of exercise circuits are shown below, one which requires little space and no equipment, and the other for a situation where there is more space and some basic equipment (a disc weight or sandbag of 20–40 lb, benches or strong chairs, a chinning bar, beam or tree branch); the actual exercises referred to are individually discussed later.

Restricted area, no equipment	*Unrestricted area, minimal equipment*
warm-up and stretch	5 minutes jogging and stretch
1. squat jumps	1. squat jumps + weight
2. press ups	2. press ups on chairs
3. back raise	3. chins or jump heaves
4. sit-ups	4. sit-ups
5. squat thrusts	5. chair step ups + weight
6. press ups (change hand position)	6. chair dips
7. toe-touching	7. lift weight (floor to overhead)
8. trunk curls	8. trunk curls
9. burpees	9. shuttle runs (10 or 20 metres)

1 minute rest, repeat 3–5 times from (1)
cool-down and stretch

2. Preliminary testing. Individuals work on the circuit at their own training levels. This is determined for each exercise (except runs) by a preliminary test of the total number of repetitions that can be performed in a minute. Adequate rest is allowed between the tests of different exercises, and within each test the repetitions need not be performed continuously; if an individual can do 30 press-ups, rest, then do another 10 within the minute, the total for the test is 40 press-ups. The actual training level for working continuously round the circuit is then half the maximum number of repetitions for each exercise (in the case given, 20 press-ups would be performed on each circuit).

3. Training sessions. In a single 20–30 minute training session, 3–5 circuits are performed. Ideally each circuit should be timed, and the 1 minute rest between circuits must be timed. Training progression is achieved by shortening the times taken to complete each circuit and by increasing the number of circuits in a session. After a month or so, the circuit should be changed, or at least the maximum repetitions for each exercise should be re-tested and the training loads adjusted accordingly.

Stage training

In this method, each exercise in the sequence is completed as an individual stage, by performing the appropriate number of repetitions, and 'sets' of repetitions, before moving on to the next exercise. Rest and recovery take place between the different sets of an exercise and between the different exercises. This method can thus have different sorts of training effects depending on the pattern and extent of the rest periods. For example, longer rest periods allow more repetitions and sets of repetitions to be done for each exercise, with consequently large effects on local strength and endurance; shorter rest periods (30 seconds) limit the number of repetitions that can be performed, but maintain a more continuously high heart rate.

Stage training is also a convenient method if large numbers of people are involved; when 20 or more team members are training together, the coach can simply carry out the general timing for the exercise and rest periods.

Technique of stage training:

1. Circuit construction. The same sorts of exercise sequences can be used for circuit training and stage training. But there are two ways of using a stage training sequence.

2. Numbered repetitions method. As in circuit training, the maximum number of repetitions is tested for each exercise. In a training session, one-third of these maximum numbers is performed as a set. For example, if 45 press-ups can be managed in a minute, then at the press-ups training station, 3–5 sets of 15 press-ups are carried out with 30 seconds rest between each set, before proceeding to the next exercise station. This method minimises local endurance requirements and continues to provide a fairly high cardiorespiratory benefit.

3. Maximum repetitions method. This method is the simplest of all, but is also the toughest in terms of local strength and endurance requirements. At each exercise station the maximum number of continuous repetitions is performed to failure, followed by a minute's rest, then again repetitions to failure (probably a lower maximum this time), another minute's rest, then a final maximum to failure (probably lower still). For example, the press-ups stage may be: 70 press-ups, rest, 55 press-ups rest, 43 press-ups. In this method each exercise is carried to the point of failure so it also provides a significant strength training effect.

Basic exercises

Individual exercises for circuit or stage training should involve as many large muscle groups as possible, in order to generate high cardiorespiratory effort. Several well known exercises that can accomplish this with the minimum of equipment are described here in relation to the four main body parts of chest-shoulders-arms, hips-legs, back, and abdomen. The actual number of exercises has been limited, in order to allow some discussion on exercise technique and variations.

Chest-shoulders-arms
Press-ups (push-ups)
Technique – The standard press-up is performed on the floor, with the body supported on the toes and arms, hands shoulder-width apart; the arms are bent until the chest touches the floor, then straightened to raise the body back to the starting position.

Comments – Short bouncing movements are of little benefit; the further the body is lowered towards the floor, the more the chest muscles are involved.

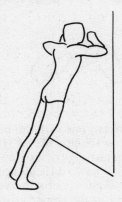

Variations – The easiest type of press-up is performed leaning against a wall. Difficulty is increased by altering the angle of the body: by doing them against, say, a table, then in the standard position on the floor, then, more difficult, with the feet at a higher level than the shoulders (say on a chair), until finally they can be done in a handstand position against a wall. A variation of the floor press-up that is particularly

useful for beginning females is that in which the body is supported on the arms and knees, rather than toes; this reduces the bodyweight that has to be raised. The emphasis placed on different muscle groups can also be varied: the chest muscles are more fully worked if the hands are supported on two chairs and the body lowered as far between them as possible;

more emphasis is put on the arms if the hands are placed close together on the floor; circling the shoulders forwards and backwards around the normal floor position of the hands, emphasises the shoulder muscles.

Dips

Technique – Dips are carried out with the body supported on parallel bars or between two chairs; the body is simply lowered and raised through as great a range of movement as possible.

Comments – This is a much more difficult upper body exercise since more of the bodyweight is being moved vertically, and more strength is required in the upper arm muscles.

Variations – The easiest type of dip is performed between two chairs with the feet resting on the floor; it is more difficult if the feet are placed on a third chair; and finally dips can be done between parallel bars with weights attached to the body.

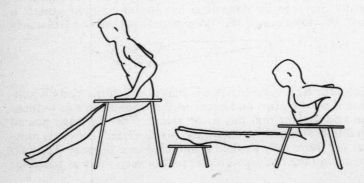

Hips-legs
Squats (deep knee bends)
Technique – With the feet shoulder-width apart, and *with the heels remaining flat on the floor throughout*, the body is lowered by bending the hips and knees until the thighs are horizontal, and then raised back to the starting position.

Comments – This exercise is useful in several respects: it exercises the hips, buttocks and thighs; if the heels remain on the floor, it stretches the hips and ankles; and because so many large muscle groups are involved, it places heavy demands on the cardiorespiratory system. However, a point to be careful about is the vulnerability of the knee joint, and uncontrolled dropping or bouncing into the lowest squat position, with the knees fully bent, should be avoided.
Variations – Some variations of the squat exercise are:
squat jumps, in which the aim is to jump as high as possible rather than simply to squat into a low position; the difficulty can be increased by clasping some kind of weight to the chest (disc weights, sandbag etc.);

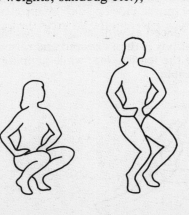

squat thrusts, in which the body is supported on the arms in the prone position while the legs are thrust out and back;

burpees, an oddly-named exercise which involves standing up between each squat thrust type of movement;

All of these exercises place great demands on the cardio-respiratory system, and one of them should be included after every third or fourth exercise in a circuit.

Lunges
Technique – The feet are placed as wide apart as possible in a front-to-back plane; the body is then lowered and raised by bending and straightening the leading leg, while keeping the rear leg as straight as possible.

Comments – This exercise has already been introduced as a groin stretching movement (page 41), but it can also be a useful strengthening exercise for the muscles of the inner thigh.

Variations – Even more emphasis is placed on the inner thighs if lunges are performed to the side. Greater effort is used by starting with the feet together, taking a large step (to the front or to the side) to sink into the low position, and then recovering to the starting position with a single push from the bent leg.

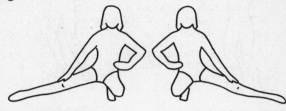

Heel raises (calf raises)

Technique – The front of the feet are supported on a raised block or book, and the heels are raised and lowered through as full a range of movement as possible; short, bouncing movements should be avoided and the exercise should be carried out at a rate that allows about 20 repetitions in a minute.

Comments – The range of movement and the muscle groups that are involved are both so limited that this exercise should not really be included in a circuit – in fact, its inclusion would actually allow so much recovery that any cardiorespiratory effects of the rest of the circuit would be lost; however, it is a very useful exercise for stretching and strengthening the calf muscles and Achilles tendons, and it can be done separately or incorporated into the rest periods between circuits; it is important to do it on a raised support so that a full range of movement can be achieved – short, bouncing heel raises can actually worsen a condition of tight calves and short Achilles tendons.

Back
Pull-ups (chins)
Technique – From a straight hanging position on a bar (or tree branch), the body is pulled up until the chin is above the bar, and then lowered completely back to the starting position.

Comments – This exercise requires so much strength in the back and arms that only individuals who are already well-developed in these areas can perform enough pull-ups at a sufficient rate to allow their inclusion in a circuit (a trained person should be able to do about 30 pull-ups in a minute).
Variations – The strength limitations can be overcome by doing each repetition with an assisting jump or heave from the floor. An easier form of the exercise can also be carried out on a lower bar by keeping the feet on the ground and raising and lowering the body at an angle of 45°.

Toe-touches

Technique – From a standing vertical position the upper body is simply bent at the hips to reach as low a position as possible, then raised to the starting position.

Comments – This simple movement exercises most of the muscles of the lower back, the buttocks and the backs of the thighs. In this context it is not necessary to keep the knees straight, nor actually to touch the toes – the aim is rather to exercise the back muscles by sweeping the body downwards and upwards. The difficulty is slightly increased by keeping the arms overhead.

Back raise (prone hyper-extensions)

Technique – In a face-down position on the floor, the upper body is raised by arching the back as strongly as possible.

Comments – This is a very useful exercise for strengthening a weak point of the body – the muscles along the spine and lower back.

Variations – The exercise is even more effective if it is performed through a greater range of movement, with the upper body projecting out from a bench or some sort of raised support (a partner is useful for holding the legs down). The difficulty is increased by holding the hands (or a weight) behind the head.

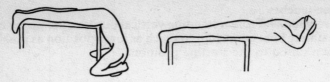

Abdomen
Sit-ups

Technique – These should be performed with bent knees and a rounded back (the head is raised off the floor first, then the shoulders, then the back).

Comments – The bent knees, rounded back technique not only helps to prevent back strain (which can result from raising the torso in a hollow-back position), but also puts more emphasis on the abdominal muscles. The muscles that are primarily responsible for the sit-up movement are actually the hip flexors (the muscles that cross the hips and attach to the thighs); these muscles are even more strongly involved when the feet are fixed under a support (which is why sit-ups are easier in that situation). More emphasis is placed on the abdominals when the hips are already flexed in the bent knees position.

Variations – In the early stages, the feet can be hooked under a support, but eventually this should be dispensed with, the heels moved ever closer to the buttocks, and the hands placed behind the head (in this position a trained individual should be able to manage around 50 sit-ups in a minute).

Trunk curls

Technique – In a back-lying position, the upper body is raised by sliding the hands as far as possible along the tops of the thighs *while keeping the small of the back on the floor*; with strong abdominal muscles, it is possible to touch the knees without the lower back leaving the floor.

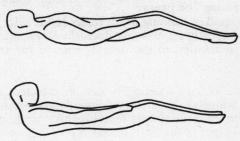

Comments – Trunk curls are a much stronger (and better) abdominal exercise than sit-ups, but for greatest effectiveness they must be performed very strictly without the lower back leaving the floor. (Abdominal exercises that involve raising the lower half of the body, rather than the upper half, are nowadays considered to be liable to provoke muscle tears and hernias; also, if the legs are held straight while they are raised, the back tends to hollow into a weak injury-prone position. Therefore any sort of **leg raises** that are done, should be performed with bent legs.)

Weight Training

The term 'weight training' may be a bit inappropriate nowadays, a more accurate name being 'progressive resistance training'. Muscles are exercised against a resistance (of which free weights are only one type) and as fitness improves, the resistance is progressively increased. This method of training has two distinct advantages.

i.) Particular muscle groups can be exercised in isolation. This is useful not only for developing some body part or other, but also for simply correcting a weakness or imbalance and for rehabilitating an injury.

ii.) Particular loads can be matched to the particular abilities of the muscles being exercised, loads greater than bodyweight being used to train large muscles, like those of the legs, and loads of less than bodyweight being used for weaker or smaller muscle groups. Furthermore, the load can be gradually increased, which makes the method extremely convenient for progression in training.

Weight training and fitness

This method of training is not really suitable for developing all aspects of fitness, and any decision about using it should be made in relation to the overall aims of the training programme.

Skinniness. Weight training is not an effective method for reducing body fat. Its energy demands are relatively low in comparison even to simple activities like walking, in which full bodyweight is moved around. (The degree of difficulty of an activity should not be confused with its actual energy requirements.) Weight training, however, can have a large influence on body shape through its effects on muscle tone.

Suppleness. Weight training can improve flexibility and muscle extensibility if exercises are performed correctly through a full range of movement. On the other hand, poor technique and limited, jerky movements can result in tighter muscles and loss of suppleness.

Stamina. Most weight training exercises are very suitable for circuit training. However, it is usually difficult to work uninterruptedly through an exercise circuit in an open session in a weights room, and cardiorespiratory fitness can be more conveniently developed by other activities. Local muscular endurance, though, can be greatly improved.

Strength. This is the aspect of fitness that is most effectively developed by weight training (and through strength, speed to a certain degree). Increase in muscle size is probably also a feature that is associated with the popular image of weight training. However, although changes in muscle tone and shape can be achieved by virtually everyone, the extent to which muscle size can be increased is largely dependent upon the individual's particular genetic make-up, and a willingness to train for over two hours a day.

The general rule of thumb in using weight training for different purposes is: 'heavy loads for strength, high repetitions for stamina, heavy loads and high repetitions for size – plus well-chosen parents.'

Equipment, jargon, and muscles
Before the actual principles of weight training are dealt with, it may be useful to explain a few somewhat technical aspects. These can be considered under the three general headings of types of equipment, terms used, and major muscle groups.

Types of equipment
There are two general types of weight training equipment: free weights and training machines.

Free weights
Description – The basic piece of equipment is the barbell, a 5–7 feet long bar on which disc weights are held by collars; the better types of barbell have a revolving sleeve or hand-grip to allow rotation of the load during movement. Short bars (8–14 inches) which also carry weights are called dumb-bells, and these are usually handled in pairs. A well-equipped training room also has benches for various exercises, racks for supporting barbells, and special boards for abdominal exercises.
Comments – The major advantages of free weights are the great variety in the types of movements that are possible with them, and the strong additional effects that their use has on other aspects of muscular control, co-ordination and balance. This also means, though, that a fair amount of instruction and practice is required, and free weights are therefore probably more suitable for an individual to whom this activity is an end in itself, rather than a means of simply preparing for another sport.

Training machines
Description – Training machines are usually large pieces of

equipment in which exercise is carried out by pushing or pulling a lever, handle or pulley, and the load can usually be changed simply by moving a peg or a screw. Because actual strength varies at different positions within a movement (see the section on how muscles work, in Chapter 3, page 92), some types of training machine cause the load against which the muscle is working also to vary during the exercise movement. Common examples of this type are the Universal multigym, where the load is varied in certain exercises by a changing lever arm, and the Nautilus training machines, where the resistance is changed by a rotating cam (itself shaped like a Nautilus shell).

Comments – Different types of machines have their own particular advantages and disadvantages. However, they all have the general features of allowing only limited types of movements, which occur only through fixed arcs. This perhaps results in a lower effectiveness on the development of muscular control and co-ordination, but it also makes for relatively safe operation with the minimum of practice and instruction. Such machines are thus more useful to the individual (or team) who is using resistance training to prepare for another sport.

Terms used in weight training

A certain amount of jargon is used in weight training, but it often allows particular situations to be described in a minimum of words.

An *exercise* is a standardised pattern of movement that trains particular muscles, and usually consists of a 'positive' (lifting) movement and a 'negative' (lowering or releasing) movement; a 'compound exercise' uses several muscle groups (deep knee bends), while a 'specific exercise' largely uses just one muscle group (heel raise, biceps curl).

A *rep* (repetition) is a single execution of an exercise, i.e. one positive lifting movement and one negative lowering movement.

A *max* (maximum) is the maximum weight that can be lifted once in a particular exercise. Thus, 10 reps of 70% max is 10 repetitions of an exercise with a weight that is 70% of the maximum that can be used in that exercise.

A *set* is a group of continuous repetitions of a single exercise. Thus, three sets of 10 repetitions each would be written 3×10.

A *schedule* is the whole plan for a training session, including the exercise sequence, and the number of sets, reps and weights used in each exercise.

The term *load* is used in more technical accounts of weight training. It is made up of two components: 'tonnage', which is the total amount of weight lifted in all the exercises, sets and reps of a single session (a measure of training quantity); and 'intensity', which is the actual weight used in any single repetition (a measure of training quality).

Major muscle groups

A certain familiarity with the major muscle groups involved in particular movements or exercises is also useful, although here, too, some jargon is used for muscle names. The muscles involved in common body movements are indicated below (the term 'prime mover' is used to describe those muscles that are primarily responsible for a movement).

Body part (muscle group)	Major functions
Shoulders (deltoids)	Raise the arms forwards, sideways or upwards; also assist in 'pressing' movements.
Chest (pectorals)	Large powerful muscles which pull the arms inwards across the chest.
Upper back (trapezius)	Base of the neck and upper back and shoulders; raises the shoulders in shrugging movements.
Back (latissimus dorsi)	Responsible for V-shape of the back; pull arms downwards towards body.
Arm, rear upper (triceps)	Straightens arms, assists deltoids and pectorals in pressing movements.
front, upper (biceps)	Bends arm, rotates forearm.
Abdominals (front and obliques)	Various groups between the ribs and the pelvis; stabilise and support the torso during movement.
Buttocks (gluteals)	Large powerful muscles which move the legs backwards and straighten the hips; prime movers in jumping and sprinting.
Hips (iliopsoas group) (hip flexors)	Extend from lower part of spine and pelvis to upper thigh; move the thighs forward and bend the hips.

Front thigh (quadriceps)	Extend from the hips to the knees; straighten the knee; prime movers in kicking and running uphill.
Rear thigh (hamstrings)	Extend from the pelvis and upper thigh to the lower leg behind the knee; curl the lower leg upwards and move the thigh backwards; prime movers in running and sprinting.
Calves (gastrocnemius-soleus group)	Extend from behind the knee and attached to the heel bone by the Achilles tendon; raise the foot up on the toes.
Shins (anterior tibialis)	Pull the foot up towards the shin.

The jargon used in muscle names is sometimes shortened even further to 'pecs', 'lats', 'glutes' etc.!

Although there is thus a fair amount of jargon, and also some complexity to muscle action, the basic principles of weight training are relatively straightforward.

Basic principles of weight training:

1. There must be some training stress. A training effect is only produced in response to a training stimulus that involves some stress or overload. That is, there must be a certain degree of effort or difficulty; effortless repetition of an exercise has little training effect.

2. The type of stress must be appropriate to the training aims. With weights there are two ways of creating a training stress – by performing a certain number of repetitions (using local muscular endurance) or by attempting to overcome a certain resistance (using strength). That is, a relatively low load (60% max) and high reps train endurance; a high load (75–100% max) and low reps train strength.

3. There must be training progression. In all forms of resistance training the basic method of progression in an exercise consists of alternating periods of progression in the number of repetitions performed, with occasions when the resistance is increased. For example, a particular resistance may just allow the completion of 15 repetitions; over successive sessions, the number of reps is pushed up to 20; at this point, the resistance is increased by about 5% and the number of repetitions reduced again to 15; training continues by pushing the reps back up to 20, and so on. For endurance training, the progression range is around 15–25 reps; for strength training it is 4–8 reps, although slightly more sophisticated systems are described later. During serious training, some form of progression (reps or weight) should be able to be achieved in virtually *every* training session – a training diary records success or laziness.

4. The exercise sequence in a training session is important. Most exercises involve the combined operation of large strong muscle groups together with weaker muscles. Thus the loads that can be handled in such compound exercises are really limited by the strengths of the weaker muscles; if these weaker muscles have already been involved in a previous exercise, their fatigue will limit the training load even more. To minimise these sorts of effects, the recommended sequence at high levels of training intensity is:

legs → chest → back → shoulders → arms → forearms → abdominals

Leg exercises are carried out first since they use the heaviest loads and involve many other muscle groups in the hips, back and even shoulders. Back exercises are inserted between chest and shoulder exercises because their 'arm-pulling' movements provide an opportunity for some arm recovery between the similar 'arm-pressing' movements for chest and shoulder training. Arm exercises come after chest and shoulders, since the weaker arm muscles already limit the training loads that the powerful chest and shoulder muscles can handle. Any forearm exercises are carried out towards the end of the session, since 'grip' is required in most other exercises. And abdominal exercises are usually performed last, since these stabilising muscles are involved in virtually all other exercises.

5. Exercises should be performed with good technique. Good technique involves carrying out each repetition through the full range of movement, with muscular control being exerted in both the positive lifting movement *and* the negative lowering movement. Such technique is required not just for safety reasons, but also as the means of obtaining the greatest training effects: a full range of movement trains a muscle over its whole range of action; it also prevents any muscle-shortening or 'tightening' effects; if swinging movements are avoided in the lifting part of an exercise, the muscle is forced to work harder; if muscular control is exerted in the lowering movement, a greater (eccentric) training effect is achieved (see the section on how muscles work, in Chapter 3, page 92). Good training technique also involves carrying out serious warm-up and cool-down routines in every training session.

The use of weights and other types of resistance training equipment can be quite dangerous, with the possibility of injury not only from actual accidents with the equipment but also from inadequate knowledge and technique. Most weight training is probably carried on outside the home, but before joining a club or gymnasium it may be useful to consider how well it measures up in the areas of safety and instruction.

General safety considerations in weight training:

1. The surroundings. Is the general area safe – firm floor with a non-slip surface and no projections?
Is there a safe training atmosphere with no horse-play?

2. The equipment. Is the equipment well-maintained?
Are the benches solid?
Are there collars for all the barbells?

3. Personal factors. Is appropriate clothing encouraged?
Is proper footwear insisted upon?
Do individuals help as catchers during lifts?
Is chewing gum banned during exercise?

4. The instruction. Are there instructors? At what times?
Do the instructors, unasked, correct poor technique?
Is a warm-up insisted upon before training?
Are stretching exercises encouraged after training?

Weight training exercises

This section simply provides a general introduction to the basic exercises and their training effects. It is not intended as a step-by-step teaching manual. Safe and effective techniques cannot be developed from just studying descriptions, no matter how explicit, and we strongly recommend that beginners obtain direct personal instruction in the early stages of a weight training programme.

The exercises are first listed below, and then described in more detail in the text (including mention of the major muscle groups involved, description of the starting and finishing positions of the exercise, comments upon points of technique, and variations that give different training effects). Where appropriate, exercises are given both for free weights and for a multigym, but it is not always possible to carry out equivalent exercises on each system – in fact, even seemingly similar exercises in the two systems may place different emphases on different muscle groups (see the text descriptions of squats and leg press).

Exercise with free weights	Exercise with multigym	Body parts involved
Power clean.		Legs, hips, back, shoulders.
Deadlift.		Legs, lower back, spine.
Squat.	Leg press.	Buttocks, hips, thighs.
	Leg extension.	Front thighs.
	Leg curls.	Rear thighs.
Heel raise.	Heel raise.	Calves.
Bench press.	Chest press.	Chest, shoulders, arms.
Dumb-bell flying.		Chest.
Pull-ups.	Lat pull-downs.	Upper back, chest, arms.
Bent-over rowing.	Seated rowing.	Upper back, arms.
Bent arm pull-overs.		Chest, upper back.
Press behind neck.	Shoulder press.	Shoulders, arms.
Dumb-bell lateral raise.		Shoulders.
Upright rowing.	Upright rowing.	Shoulders, upper back, arms.
Shoulder shrugs.	Shoulder shrugs.	Neck, upper back.
Biceps curl.	Biceps curl.	Front upper arms.
Triceps press.	Lat push-down.	Rear upper arms.
Sit-ups + weights.	Sit-ups + incline.	Hip flexors, abdominals.
Trunk curls.	Trunk curls.	Abdominals.

Power clean (barbell, firm floor)
Muscles – quadriceps, hips, gluteals, back, shoulder girdle.
Technique – feet under the barbell, heels on the floor, hands shoulder-width apart, overhand grasp, *back flat but not vertical*; straighten the legs and hips explosively to bring the barbell to shoulder height, then dip slightly and rotate the elbows forward to catch the bar in the rest position on the front

shoulders; return the barbell in two movements through the hang position to the floor.

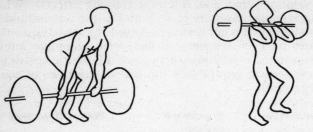

Comments – a useful all-round exercise; with light weights, a good warm-up movement; with high reps, a good cardiorespiratory conditioner; but beginners should not pursue this exercise without correct technique.

Deadlift (barbell, firm floor)
Muscles – legs, hips, back, spine, shoulder girdle, hand grip.
Technique – same starting position as for power clean; strongly lift the barbell until the body is fully erect in the front hang position; *keep the back flat throughout*; return the barbell to the floor under control.

Comments – this exercise is carried out with heavier weights than for the power clean; it is useful for developing overall body strength, but can lead to a loss of explosive speed; it also is an exercise that should not be pursued without correct technique.
Variations – a mixed handgrip (over and under grasps) stops a·heavy barbell from rolling out of the hands; the **stiff-legged deadlift** is a quite different and much more dangerous exercise

in which the legs are not involved and all the emphasis is placed on the lower back muscles, and which should not be attempted at all by a novice.

Squats (barbell and stands; two catchers also advised)
Muscles – lower back, hips, buttocks, thighs; also a good cardiorespiratory conditioner (because it involves many large muscle groups); also develops suppleness in the hips and ankles.
Technique – feet shoulder-width apart and turned slightly outwards, bar resting on the back of the shoulders (not the neck); keep the heels on the floor and bend the knees and hips until the thighs are parallel to the ground, pause, and return to the start position; keep the head up and back flat.

Comments – this is the best all-round lower body exercise, but another one which needs instruction to develop the correct technique; for knee safety it is important not to collapse into the lowest position with a bounce; and the back should not lean too far forward (hip suppleness is needed to keep the hips over the feet, rather than become pushed backwards).
Variations – **half-squats** (not going right down into the low position) allow heavier weights to be handled, and are a safer and equally effective exercise for the leg movements required in most sports; **front squats** (with the barbell held in the rest position on the front shoulders) place greater emphasis on the quadriceps.

Leg press (multigym)
Muscles – quadriceps, buttocks.
Technique – seated at the leg press station; forcefully extend the legs, pause, recover to the start position.

Comments – the seat should be adjusted for the appropriate range of movement, but the legs should not be bent under load through more than a right angle (for knee joint safety); a greater training effect is obtained if the legs are not allowed to fully lock out (which allows momentary muscle recovery); this is not such a massive lower body exercise as the squat, and the cardiorespiratory system is not so stressed (the seated position means that the hips and lower back are not so heavily involved).

Leg extension (multigym)
Muscles – quadriceps.
Technique – seated at the exercise station, insteps hooked under the bottom set of rollers; fully straighten the legs, pause, lower to the start position.

Comments – an exercise for the muscles that support the knee joint and therefore very useful for runners and games players; it must be carried out with control (kicking or swinging up a huge weight by its own momentum may be ego-boosting, but it does not exercise any muscles and it can damage the knee joint); it is also important to straighten the knee fully (only at this point are the 'knee muscles' brought into play).

Leg curl (multigym)
Muscles – hamstrings.
Technique – face-down at the exercise station, heels hooked

under the top set of rollers and knees just off the bench; fully bend the legs upwards, pause, and lower to the start position.

Comments – muscular balance between the antagonist muscles involved in leg extensions and leg curls is important in avoiding thigh injuries; the resistance used for leg curls should be around 60% of that for leg extensions.

Heel raise (barbell, dumb-bells or multigym)
Muscles – calves (gastrocnemius, soleus).
Technique – as for heel raise in free body exercise; extra resistance is added by supporting a barbell or dumb-bells, or by grasping the handles of a multigym chest press station.
Comments – it is important to have the front parts of the feet on a raised block to allow a full range of movement; also, avoid using heavy weights that cause short bouncing movements.

Bench press (barbell, bench, stands; at least one catcher advised)
Muscles – pectorals, deltoids, triceps.
Technique – face-up on the bench, feet flat on the floor, arms fully extended, hands slightly more than shoulder-width apart; lower the barbell to the chest, then press it forcefully back to the start position.

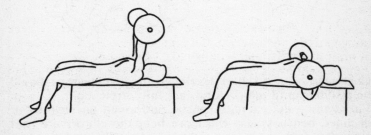

Comments – this is the basic upper body weights exercise, and is equivalent to the press-up; to involve the pectorals fully, it is important to touch the chest with the barbell in every rep, but for safety it should not be bounced off the chest; the buttocks should not arch off the bench.

Variations – a wide grasp emphasises the pectorals, a narrow grasp emphasises the triceps; an inclined 45° bench emphasises the upper part of the pectorals, a declined 30° bench (head downwards) emphasises the lower chest; all of these movements can also be performed with dumb-bells; the **chest press station** of the multigym trains the same muscle groups, but without the variations allowed by free weights.

Dumb-bell flying (dumb-bells, bench)
Muscles – pectorals.
Technique – face-up on the bench, arms extended vertically with the elbows slightly bent; lower the arm sideways and downwards as far as possible, without changing the angle of the elbow, pause and recover to the start position.

Comments – a good chest developer; the first few reps should be cautious until the pectorals are fully stretched.
Variations – the exercise can be performed on inclined or declined benches; also the more bent the elbows are (not more than 90°), the more weight can be handled and the more emphasis is placed on the pectorals; the straighter the elbows, the greater the strain on the shoulder joint.

Pull-up (chinning bar or multigym)
Muscles – latissimus, pectorals, biceps.
Technique – hanging from the bar, overhand grasp (palms facing away); pull the body up to chin over the bar and lower to the start position.

Comments – the lowering movement should be controlled and to full arm extension.
Variations – an underhand grasp (palms facing the body) makes the exercise easier since the biceps are more involved; the exercise is more difficult and the lat muscles receive more emphasis in **rear pull-ups** (overhand grasp, and the back of the neck touches the bar); all of these variations can be performed seated or kneeling at the **lat pull-down** station of the multigym.

Bent-over rowing (barbell, dumb-bells, or multigym)
Muscles – latissimus, biceps.
Technique – body bent forward at the waist, *back flat* (by thrusting the chest out), knees slightly bent, overhand grasp slightly greater than shoulder-width; pull the bar up to touch the chest, pause and lower to the start position (not to the floor).

Comments – the back must be kept flat throughout, and the elbows kept high; the bar should be pulled to the chest, not to the stomach, and it should be lowered under control.
Variations – the exercise can be performed with one or with two dumb-bells; the forehead can be supported on a bench; the same muscle groups are exercised in **seated rowing** at the low pulley station on a multigym.

Bent arm pull-over (bench, barbell or dumb-bell)
Muscles – pectorals, latissimus, muscles of the rib-cage.
Technique – face-up on the bench, head over the edge of the bench, barbell in a narrow over-grasp resting on the rib-cage; lower the barbell to the floor in a semi-circular movement, passing *close to the face*, and recover through the same close arc to the start position.

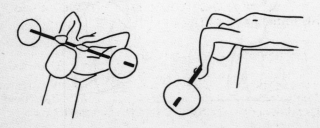

Comments – do not confuse this exercise with **straight arm pull-overs**, which are carried out with much lighter weights and which do not work the lats so strongly.
Variations – the exercise can be performed with a dumb-bell clasped vertically between the hands.

Press behind neck (bench, barbell or multigym)
Muscles – rear deltoids, trapezius, triceps.
Technique – seated with the barbell resting behind the neck, hands comfortably more than shoulder-width, feet secure under the bench; press the barbell to full arm extension, pause and lower to the start position.

Comments – the exercise is performed seated in order to place more emphasis on the shoulders; do not lean backwards (this is a form of cheating, since the strong pectorals become involved).
Variations – the **military press** is performed with a narrower grip in front of the head and involves the front deltoids and the pectorals; the use of dumb-bells requires more muscular control; the exercise can be performed on the **shoulder press** station of the multigym, facing outwards (back muscles) or inwards to the machine (pectorals).

Dumb-bell lateral raise (dumb-bells)
Muscles – deltoids.
Technique – standing, arms downwards, palms inwards; raise the dumb-bells sideways and upwards to shoulder height, pause and lower under control to the start position.

Comments – the palms must face downwards throughout the movement (turning them to the front or upwards is a form of cheating since the stronger front deltoids and pectorals are recruited).

Upright rowing (barbell or multigym)
Muscles – trapezius, deltoids, biceps.
Technique – standing, arms downwards in front of the body, narrow over-grasp; pull the barbell upwards to the chin, pause and lower under control to the start position.

Comments – the elbows must be kept above the bar and the bar must reach the chin (it is only at this final point of the movement that the trapezius muscles are fully involved); do not lean forward or duck the chin.
Variations – the exercise can be performed with the T-bar at the low pulley station of the multigym.

Shoulder shrugs (barbell, dumb-bells or multigym)
Muscles – trapezius.

Technique – standing, arms downwards, shoulder-width over-grasp; raise the shoulders as high as possible without bending the arms, pause and *slowly* lower to the start position.

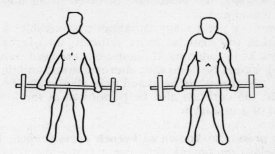

Comments – the full range of shoulder movement must be achieved on every rep (better too light than too heavy a weight).
Variations – the exercises can be performed with two dumb-bells or by gripping the chest press station of the multigym; an alternative movement involves rolling the shoulders backwards and forwards (still with as high elevation as possible).

Curl (barbell, dumb-bells or multigym)
Muscles – biceps.
Technique – standing, arms fully extended downwards, shoulder-width underhand grasp; bend the arms to raise the barbell close to the chest to the fully contracted position, pause and slowly lower *to the full arms extended start position.*

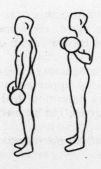

Comments – do not bring the elbows forward at any part of the movement; do not lean backwards or swing the upper body (stricter curls can be done seated, or with the back against a wall); the biceps are involved in all upper body pulling movements.

Variations – a great many variations are possible; a narrow grip makes the exercise more difficult; an overhand grip emphasises the forearms; if dumb-bells are used, raising and lowering should be done with alternate arms, and during the upward movement the hand and wrist should also be rotated upwards; the curl can also be performed at the low pulley position of a multigym.

Triceps press also known as **French press** (bench, barbell, dumb-bell or multigym)

Muscles – triceps.

Technique – face upwards, head on the bench, arms extended vertically, narrow overhand grasp; without changing the position of the upper arms, bend the elbows until the barbell touches the forehead, then straighten the arms to the start position.

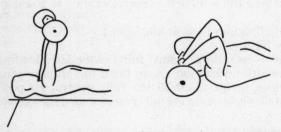

Comments – do not confuse this exercise with bent arm or straight arm pull-overs; here, the upper arms must be kept vertical throughout; the triceps are involved in all upper body pressing movements.

Variations – the least satisfactory variation is performed in a standing position with the upper arms vertical (the shoulder joint is then in a fully extended and weak situation); the triceps are strongly exercised in **lat push-downs** on the multigym; with a narrow overgrasp and *with the elbows kept firmly against the sides throughout the exercise*, straighten the arms against resistance, then slowly return to the start position.

Forearms: for general purposes, the forearms are exercised by the grip that is required in most weight training movements; there are special forearm exercises (**wrist curls, wrist rolling**), but for any special development of grip strength or endurance (say for racquet sports) it is doubtful whether the relatively few reps (30?) of wrist exercises that are likely to be performed in a training session, are as effective as simply squeezing something like a squash ball periodically throughout the day.

Sit-ups (abdominal board, disc weights)
Muscles – hip flexors, abdominals.
Technique – face-up on the board, knees bent, feet supported, arms folded or (more difficult) hands behind the head; raise the upper body in a curling movement until the elbows touch the knees, and lower under control to the start position.

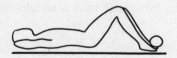

Comments – the hip flexors and upper thighs provide great assistance; the degree of difficulty should be increased whenever 40–50 reps can be achieved.
Variations – the difficulty is increased by progressively inclining the abdominal board, or by holding a weight on the chest or behind the head.

Trunk curls (disc weights)
Muscles – abdominals.
Technique – face-up, legs straight, buttocks tucked well under so that the small of the back touches the floor; try to touch the knees with the finger tips *while the small of the back stays on the floor.*

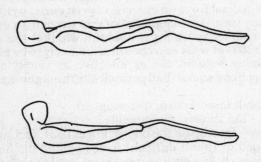

Comments – this is a much tougher exercise than sit-ups when performed correctly; the small of the back must remain on the floor and reps are carried out at around 30 per minute.
Variations – the difficulty is increased with a weight on the chest.

Weight training programmes
In this section, weight training routines for different purposes are described. These include routines for general training, and examples of routines for preparing for other sports activities.

A basic programme
In any kind of programme, the key feature should be simplicity. There are no magic exercises and there are no particular benefits to be gained from cramming a great variety

of different exercises into a training session – any 'magic' comes from the technique with which the exercises are carried out, and from the progression in performance that is achieved. Examples of exercise routines are given below, both for multi-gym and free weights; Free Weights Routine (2) simply has a few more difficult exercises.

Body part	Multigym	Free weights (1)	Free weights (2)
Legs.	Leg press. Leg extension. Leg curl.	Squat.	Power clean. Front squat.
Chest.	Chest press.	Bench press.	Incline bench press. Dumb-bell flying.
Back.	Lat pull-down.	Bent-over rowing.	Pull-ups.
Shoulders.	Shoulder press.	Press behind neck.	Press behind neck. Upright rowing.
Arms, front rear.	Biceps curl. Lat push-down.	Biceps curl. Triceps press.	Dumb-bell curl. Parallel bar dips.
Abdominals.	Incline sit-ups.	Weighted sit-ups.	Trunk curls.

Notes on basic training methods:

1. A basic programme should lay a foundation of both endurance (from the number of reps) and strength (from getting close to the point of muscle failure in each set). This can be done by using loads around 70% max, and working in the range of 10–15 reps.

2. Some form of progression should be apparent in virtually every training session. An exercise is first carried out with a load that just barely allows the completion of 10 reps; over subsequent sessions, the reps are pushed up to 15, at which point the load is increased by 5% and 10 reps started again.

3. Three sets of an exercise should be performed in each session, and in this type of training it doesn't really matter whether the 3 sets of an exercise are all completed before moving on to the next, or whether 1 set is done at a time and the whole sequence gone round 3 times (probably the more continuous training in the second method is less time-consuming).

4. Schedules that are aimed more specifically at strength training use greater loads and lower numbers of repetitions, and in

this type of training all the sets of an exercise are completed before moving on to the next.

5. This sort of basic training programme should be carried out 3 times a week, for 2–3 months.

Advanced methods

In more advanced forms of strength training it is not the actual types of exercises that change, but rather the techniques of training and the patterns of reps and sets.

Forced reps. These are also called negative reps. A training partner assists in the positive lifting movement of the exercise, but the individual alone exerts maximum resistive force during the lowering movement. Forced reps can be carried out either as a few more assisted repetitions after the point of failure in a normal training set, or by specifically using a supra-maximal load to perform a few negative repetitions – either way, such intense training techniques should not be over-used.

Pyramid sets. An exercise starts with a basal set of reps (say 6 at 75% max) and then progresses through further sets of increasing weight and decreasing reps (say ×5, ×4, ×3, ×2) up to a single repetition at around 100% max; additional training can be obtained by working back through decreasing weight and increasing reps. Pyramid sets are usually performed only with the major compound exercises (power clean, squat, deadlift, shoulder presses and the various forms of bench press).

Pre-exhaust training (also called the multi-set system). As already indicated in the discussion on exercise sequence, the training loads of the major compound exercises are really limited by the strengths of the weakest muscle groups involved in the exercise. This means that the larger, stronger groups can remain under-trained (in all the 'pressing' types of exercises for the upper body, the relative weakness of the arm triceps limits the loads that can be put on the stronger chest or shoulder groups). The pre-exhaust system is an attempt to overcome this situation by performing pairs of exercises as a 'multi-set' with no rest between the individual exercises; that is, the larger muscle group is 'pre-exhausted' by a specific exercise before the compound exercise is carried out. It is very important that there be as little lag time as possible between the exercises of a multi-set, since a muscle recuperates much of its strength within two or three seconds. Examples of multi-set pairs of exercises are shown below.

Body part	Specific exercise for the major muscle group	Compound exercise for all muscle groups
legs	leg extension (quadriceps)	→ squats or leg press
chest	dumb-bell flying (pectorals)	→ bench press
back	bent arm pull-over (lats)	→ pull-ups or lat pull-downs
shoulders	lateral raise (deltoids)	→ press behind neck

Super-set system. This is at first glance similar to multi-sets, but the training aim is different: in multi-sets the aim is to train the same muscle group in consecutive exercises; in super-sets the aim is to train different muscle groups of the same body part. For example, biceps curls for the front of the upper arm and triceps presses for the rear of the arm may be performed as a super-set, in order to stimulate the overall metabolism, blood flow and development of the whole upper arm.

Finally, attempts to increase muscle size substantially require large increases in the sheer volume of training, generally accomplished by increasing the number of sets in each exercise to anything from 6 to 12. By this stage, training is usually also on a daily basis, using some kind of split schedule (lower body one day, upper body the next; or heavy compound exercises one day, specific exercises the next).

Weight training for particular activities

The first point to be made here is that weight training cannot substitute for actual activity-related training; training effects are specific and preparations for a particular activity must involve that activity to a large degree. Weight training, therefore, should be looked on as something that enables more effective games-training to be carried out. The second point is that, with the exception of so-called 'assistance exercises' for competitive weight-lifting and for certain athletic events, it is misleading to think that there are special exercises for different sports. The standard weight training exercises are the most effective, and any differences between the preparations for different sports derive simply from the ways in which the exercises are used.

With these qualifications in mind, weight training is useful to other activities in several ways:

1. For overall body conditioning in strength and stamina;
2. For improvement of features *not* directly developed by the sport itself;
3. For improvement of features that *are* directly required in the sport;
4. For protection against, and to aid recovery from, injury.

Preparations for different types of sports place different degrees of emphasis on each of these general points, and this is illustrated below with reference to selected activities.

Endurance sports. An individual who is already spending a great deal of time running or cycling can gain little from weight training in terms of aim (3), but could probably benefit from attention to aims (2) and (4). For example, a distance runner already spending over an hour a day on intense leg activity isn't going to gain further useful leg strength or stamina from 10 minutes of special leg exercises; but he or she would greatly benefit from the use of weights to correct the likely muscular imbalances in legs that do so much running. They would probably also benefit from a limited amount of upper body endurance work. An example of such a schedule is shown below:

Body part	Training aims	Exercises	Comments
Upper body.	Development of general muscular endurance.	1. Bench press. 2. Bent-over rowing. 3. Press behind neck. 4. Upright rowing.	Light weights, sets of 15–25 reps for all exercises.
Trunk.	Development of strength and endurance for trunk stability.	5. Sit-ups. 6. Prone hyper-extensions.	Feet supported*. Face-down on bench, feet held by partner.
Legs.	Correction of muscular imbalance.	7. Leg extensions.	No swinging movements, pause at full leg extension.
		8. Leg curls.	Use 60% leg extension weight.
		9. Heel raises.	Raised support, no bounce.

*If the insteps are hooked under some support, then the shin muscles that are under-used in running also get some exercise.

Games. When weights are used to help in games preparations, the aims of general body conditioning and protection from injury are always of prime importance. For example, the basis for the specimen schedules shown below for games like soccer and hockey is that:

1. Performance in most games is improved by greater general strength and muscular endurance in the upper and lower body;

2. All games that involve vigorous changes in direction place great strain on the knees, and leg extension exercises give a great deal of protection:

Game	Body part	Training aims	Exercises	Comments
Soccer, hockey, etc.	Upper body.	Strength-endurance from the basic upper body exercises.	1. Bench press. 2. Bent-over rowing. 3. Shoulder press. 4. Upright rowing.	All exercises sets of 8–12 reps with 70–80% max.
	Abdominals.		5. Sit-ups.	Sets of 30 reps.
	Legs.	Strength-endurance. Groin suppleness. Knee protection.	6. Half-squats. 7. Lunges – front and sideways. 8. Leg extensions.	Sets of 20 reps. Light weights, pause at full leg extensions.

In certain situations, weights can be used directly to develop the special features that are required in a game. For example, in rugby there are special requirements for strength, particularly in 'pulling' movements with the upper body and 'pushing' movements with the lower body. The weight training schedule shown below reflects these requirements.

Game	Body part	Training aims	Exercises	Comments
Rugby.	Upper body.	Strength, especially in pulling movements.	1. Dumb-bell flying. 2. Bent-over rowing. 3. Shoulder shrugs. 4. Pull-ups.	Sets of 8–12 reps, each set to failure.

Game	Body part	Training aims	Exercises	Comments
Rugby.	Mid-body.	Strength.	5. Sit-ups.	Sets of 20 reps with 20kg on chest.
			6. Prone hyper-extensions for back muscles.	Sets of 20 reps with 20kg behind head.
	Lower body.	Strength.	7. Power cleans. 8. Squats. 9. Deadlifts.	Pyramid sets to maximum.

As another example of special training requirements, racquet or club games like tennis, squash, badminton, golf, all require muscular endurance in the forearms and shoulder girdle.

Game	Body part	Training aims	Exercises	Comments
Tennis, squash, badminton, golf.	Upper body.	Endurance in the neck, shoulders and forearms.	1. Bench press. 2. Upright rowing. 3. Shoulder press. 4. Lateral raise. 5. Shoulder shrugs.	Sets of 15–25 reps.
			6. Wrist rolling.	For 5 minutes continuously.
	Abdominals.		7. Sit-ups.	Sets of 30 reps.
	Legs.	Strength-endurance. Groin suppleness. Knee protection.	8. Half-squats. 9. Lunges. 10. Leg extensions.	Sets of 20 reps. Sets of 30 reps.

Finally, however, it should be borne in mind that the primary requirement for most physical games is aerobic fitness, an aspect that is not greatly developed by weight training. That is, all fitness training programmes for games should be based around the fast-paced aerobic run.

3

BODY BASICS: THE EXERCISING BODY

Training is usually carried out more effectively, and more enthusiastically, if it is based upon some understanding of the body processes and events that underlie physical activity. This chapter tries to give a general working knowledge of the exercising body.

The body can be regarded as a system of levers, the bones, which are moved by the actions of their attached muscles. All movement results entirely from muscle contraction, brought about by the effects of a special form of chemical energy on the muscle tissue itself. Therefore, any consideration of the background to movement and exercise involves two aspects: the direct provision of energy to the muscles, and the actions of the muscles in moving their bony levers. (Eventually, of course, energy must be taken into the body itself, and nutrition in relation to training is discussed later.)

How Muscles Get Energy

The blood system is responsible for supplying all the nutritional requirements of a muscle and for removing its waste products. In the short term, oxygen is the most significant factor supplied by the blood. The whole system involved in the uptake and absorption of oxygen, and in its delivery to the muscles is referred to as the *cardiorespiratory system* (or sometimes, the cardiovascular-pulmonary system), and includes the heart, the lungs, the blood and all the blood vessels and capillaries. The total capacity of the cardiorespiratory system can be markedly different between individuals, although, as outlined in the section on stamina in Chapter 1, the capacity of all the components in the system can be increased with training.

Energy sources

The chemical that causes a muscle to contract is produced within the actual muscle itself and can be processed from stored carbohydrate, fat or protein, depending on the circumstances. For example, under conditions of starvation, body protein is digested to provide muscle energy. Again, during activity of very long duration, fat may be utilised. However, in normal circumstances the major part of muscle energy is obtained from carbohydrate. This is stored as *glycogen*, which simply consists of long chains of glucose sugar and is very similar to plant starches; when energy is required, the stored glycogen is broken down to its constituent sugar units for processing. In the short term, the glycogen supply for a particular muscle is stored within that muscle. (Although the liver carries the largest single store of glycogen in the body, the bulk of this is used to supply energy, as blood sugar, to the brain.) The glycogen in a muscle can account for 1–2% of the muscle's total weight, enough to supply energy for over an hour of continuous activity. In an untrained individual, the inability to maintain activity is not so much due to a shortage of stored energy, but rather to the inability to process or utilise sufficient energy. In endurance-trained athletes like marathon runners, however, whose oxygen-supply and energy-processing systems are of great capacity, the amount of glycogen can be a limiting factor. The size of a muscle's glycogen store can be increased to a certain degree, but this must involve subjecting *that particular muscle* to a period of appropriate endurance training. (One implication of all this is that there are no energy-related reasons for eating something immediately before a sports event that only lasts for an hour or two – the body cannot process the food in time, and anyway the energy is not required. Such a snack may even be counter-productive since it drives the body's metabolism into an expectant energy-storing, rather than energy-releasing, mode.)

Energy processing

The biochemical machinery that actually provides the muscle with energy is also located within the muscle. Each muscle has three different types of energy-processing systems, with rather cumbersome names, which supply the muscle with different amounts of energy in different situations.

1. The *anaerobic alactic system* uses a special non-glycogen store of energy (called creatine phosphate) which can provide the muscle with energy virtually instantaneously, without needing oxygen; it is really the muscle's emergency system. But, creatine phosphate is stored in very small amounts, and can only sustain very short bursts of activity for about 1–5 seconds. Also, training cannot increase the muscle's store of creatine phosphate to any significant extent.

2. The *anaerobic lactic system* can also supply the muscle with energy in the absence of oxygen, but it uses glycogen and, because of the lack of oxygen, the waste product lactic acid is formed. Intense activity of a muscle causes this system to operate at a high level, until eventually the build-up of lactic acid inhibits the muscle's action. The blood system removes lactic acid to the liver for detoxification, and during a recovery period the muscle regains its ability to function. The length of time for which this system can support all-out work by a muscle is around 30 seconds; appropriate types of (anaerobic) training can extend this to around 40 seconds.

3. The *aerobic system* of energy provision within a muscle utilises oxygen and thus interacts with the cardiorespiratory system. The presence of oxygen in the muscle allows stored foodstuffs (primarily glycogen, but also protein or fat if necessary) to be transformed into muscle energy by a series of reactions which avoid the production of lactic acid. This aerobic process can therefore continue for as long as the energy demands of the muscle are within the capacities of the oxygen delivery system and the food store. Appropriate training can increase the capacities of all the components in the aerobic system, i.e. the oxygen delivery system, the aerobic machinery within the muscle itself, and the size of the glycogen store.

The extents to which the aerobic and anaerobic systems contribute to energy provision depends upon both the intensity of activity and the aerobic capacity of the muscle; as soon as exercise intensity exceeds aerobic capacity, the anaerobic system supplements the energy supply, a situation usually accompanied by the breathlessness of oxygen shortage. It takes several hours for lactic acid to be removed from the muscle and resynthesised to glycogen, perhaps even as long as 24 hours after intensely anaerobic activity. Therefore, while the breathless operation of the anaerobic system is fairly obvious, a less obvious feature is the gradual build-up of lactic acid that can occur in the longer term if the recovery time between highly anaerobic training sessions, or events, is insufficient. In this case, the effects are not so dramatic, but still result in poor muscle function and performance – in other words, over-training.

The anaerobic system is not only limited in the duration for which it can sustain muscle activity, it is also extremely inefficient. In comparison to the aerobic system it produces less than 6% of actual muscle energy from the same amount of glycogen. Therefore although anaerobic fitness is necessary for certain specialised athletic events (e.g. 400 metres running), development of the aerobic system is much more useful for general fitness purposes.

How Muscles Work

There are three different types of muscle in the human body:

smooth muscle is responsible for the automatic movements of many of the body's internal organs, such as blood vessels and intestines;

cardiac muscle drives the pumping action of the heart;

skeletal muscle is attached to bone, and its actions bring about all the voluntary movements of the body.

Muscles and bones

Skeletal muscles are generally attached across at least one joint, and are connected to their appropriate bones either by a *tendon* (usually on the more movable lever of the joint) or by direct attachment. Other connective tissues, *ligaments*, also cross and stabilise the joint. Muscle contraction thus alters the relative positions of the two levers of the joint, and all body movements result from this shortening or pulling action of muscle. That is, muscles do not 'push'; any pushing or straightening movement of a limb is brought about by the contraction of another set of muscles. Within a single simple movement such as bending the arm, different muscle groups are involved in different ways: the muscle at the front of the upper arm, the biceps, contracts; simultaneously the triceps at the rear of the arm must lengthen, and is thus called the *antagonist* of this movement. During arm straightening, the triceps contracts and the biceps is the lengthening antagonist. The involvement of antagonistic muscle groups in many movements is important to training practices in at least two respects. It means that muscles should be progressively stretched in a warm-up, so that sudden powerful contractions don't tear the antagonistic muscles of a movement. It also means that the strengths of antagonistic muscles must be suitably matched; if one group is too weak, it is vulnerable to injury from the strong actions of its antagonistic group. For example, over-development of the quadriceps muscles on the front of the thigh can result in damage to the hamstrings at the rear of the thigh (a situation remedied by an appropriate balance of leg curl and leg extension exercises on a multigym).

Muscles and muscle fibres

A cross-section through a muscle shows it to be extremely fibrous (see Fig. 3). The basic structural unit inside a muscle is the *muscle fibre*. These fibres are bound together into larger bundles, through which run blood vessels and nerves. The fibres themselves are composed of smaller fibrils, and each fibril is packed with even smaller filaments of muscle protein. A feature crucial to muscle action is that these ultimate protein filaments are arranged in a highly overlapping way (see Fig. 3). Muscle contraction results from the protein filaments pulling themselves over each other in a ratchet-like fashion, to overlap even further; this shortening effect is transmitted up through the various levels of fibres, the muscle contracts across its joint and a limb moves. The ratchet interaction of the protein filaments is caused by the effects of the muscle energy chemical mentioned earlier. (The glycogen stores and the energy-processing machineries are also carried in the muscle fibres.)

Different types of muscle fibres have been distinguished, and have received the popular (though misleading) names of *fast twitch* and *slow twitch* fibres. Fast twitch fibres are thick, and have highly developed anaerobic systems. These fibres come into operation during explosive muscle actions. The thinner slow twitch fibres have aerobic energy-processing systems, and seem to be responsible for low intensity-long duration activities. It has become popular knowledge that the proportions of such fibre types in an individual are determined by inheritance, and that power athletes have high proportions

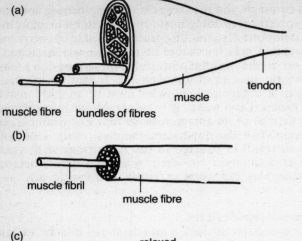

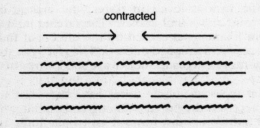

Fig. 3 Diagrams of different levels of muscle structure.
    (a) A muscle, made up of bundles of muscle fibres.
    (b) A muscle fibre, made up of smaller muscle fibrils.
    (c) A muscle fibril, which contains two types of overlapping protein
        filaments that slide over each other to bring about muscle
        contraction.

of the fast twitch fibres, while endurance athletes have large amounts of slow twitch fibres. There is an element of truth in this, but the full significance of muscle fibre type is by no means clear yet; new sub-types are still being identified, and the effects of training on the different types are being studied.

Muscle contraction

Skeletal muscle must receive a nerve impulse to trigger off the filament-sliding events that are the basis of muscle contraction. A single nerve cell can, through branching, control several muscle fibres. A group of muscle fibres and their controlling nerve is called a *motor unit*, and each muscle consists of many such units. Contraction occurs only in the fibres of motor units which have been directly activated by nerve impulses; and all the fibres activated by a nerve impulse contract completely – there is no partial contraction of a muscle fibre. Therefore, the force of a muscle contraction is directly related to the number of motor units recruited and fired during the movement; a single maximum effort requires recruitment of the greatest possible number of motor units; more refined movements require the co-ordinated deployment of units. Thus strength involves appropriate nerve-muscle interaction, and strength training, like skill, also benefits from practice of the actual movements for which the strength is required.

Besides being the means by which instructions are conveyed to the muscle, nerves are also involved in relaying information from the muscle. *Sensory nerves* within the muscle provide various sorts of information about the state of the muscle, in order that appropriate action may be initiated. For example, there are sensory nerves in the muscle tendon whose actions 'damp down' the force of contraction and thus protect the muscle against possible over-contraction. Part of any strength-training effect is thought to arise from a reduction in this damping mechanism, through increased shielding of these sensory nerves in tendon connective tissue that has been thickened by training (and an ability to override this protective mechanism in moments of crisis may be the basis for unusual feats of strength). Again, there are other sensory nerves within the muscle called stretch sensors, which monitor the extent to which the muscle is being stretched and which, if necessary, initiate more contraction to protect the muscle against overstretching. This protective stretch reflex contraction of a muscle is the reason for avoiding jerky bouncing movements in stretching exercises (the sudden stretches may actually induce a degree of muscle contraction).

Although muscles can exert force only by contracting, the contraction can occur under different circumstances, a feature that has some significance for various aspects of training. (The terms used to refer to different aspects of muscle contraction may seem cumbersome initially, but once familiar, can describe fairly complex situations in the minimum of words.) In the first place muscle length can change, or not:

i.   an *isotonic* contraction ('equal tension') is one in which the tension in the muscle is kept fairly constant while the muscle length changes; this really describes any normal limb movement against a constant load;

ii.   an *isometric* contraction ('equal length') is one in which the muscle length does not change; the muscle contracts against an immovable resistance and there is no limb movement;

iii. an *isokinetic* contraction ('equal speed') is one in which there is change in muscle length, but the load also varies throughout the movement; this type of contraction is fairly uncommon and is seen in swimming (the harder the water is pushed, the harder it pushes back).

Full development of force in each of these types of contraction requires different methods of training (particular systems are described in Chapter 1, in the strength section, page 16).

Secondly, when the muscle changes in length during a movement, it alternately gets longer and shorter:

iv.   a *concentric* contraction occurs when the muscle is shortening during a pulling movement, e.g. the biceps muscle contracts concentrically while the forearm is being raised;

v.   an *eccentric* contraction occurs when the muscle is lengthening during a ('negative') lowering movement, e.g. the biceps contracts eccentrically while the bent arm is lowering a weight.

Thus, in any training exercise the lowering movement has as important a training effect as the lifting movement. In fact, many authorities maintain that the eccentric contractions are more effective for strength training, and advocate 'negative reps' in which extra-heavy loads are lowered using maximum resistance (the idea is that during such negative movements, progressively fewer fibres are involved in maintaining resistance).

Thirdly, 'strength' varies markedly over the range of a limb's movement – weightlifters are familiar with the so-called sticking points of lifts and exercises:

vi.   the changing *efficiencies of leverage*, as the limbs alter position around the joint, account for part of this variation;

vii. the *muscle power curve* is also involved; this is the actual force that the muscle itself can exert, and it is different at different muscle lengths; the effect is thought to arise from differences in the degree of overlap among the protein filaments inside the muscle. (When the muscle is stretched, there is little filament overlap and therefore a smaller ratchet effect; when it is contracted, there is so much overlap that individual filaments may interfere with each other.)

Recognition of this variation in strength at different positions within a movement has had a great influence on the design of modern training equipment, in which various mechanical principles (levers, cams or pistons) are used to change the load deliberately within an exercise movement.

Food And Fitness

The energy value of food is measured in terms of the amount of heat that would be liberated by its complete combustion. The same units are used to express the amounts of energy required to carry out particular activities. The official unit of the system is now the joule (J), although the *Calorie* may be more familiar to most people. (1 nutritional Calorie = 1000 heat calories or 1 kilocalorie; to convert calories to joules, and kcal to kJ, multiply by 4.18.)

Exercise and energy requirements

Interest in the calorie values of foods or in the energy used in different activities generally stems from an interest in losing weight. At first glance, the energy budget of exercise seems fairly bleak – most activities have to be carried out for absurdly long times in order to use up significant amounts of fat. However, the point is that the activity doesn't have to be continuous. The same number of calories are used whether the same total activity covers one session or many shorter sessions; three games of tennis a week would remove a pound of fat in less than three weeks, without any change in diet. (Conversely, of course, regular intake of even a small amount of extra energy is equally effective at putting on fat; an *excess* of 100 kcals per day, about one fifth of a chocolate bar (weighing 100g), would result in 9 lb of fat in a year.)

Energy used in different activities*

	No. of kcal lost per hour	Time in hours to lose 1 lb of fat†
Sleeping	70	57
Sitting	105	38
Walking	300	13
Tennis	430	10
Swimming	430	10
Cycling	450	9
Jogging	750	5.3
Running	1200	3.3

*Generalised values based around a 12 stone male; lighter individuals use less energy.
†1 lb fat = 4000 kcals.

Another point concerns the intensity of activity, an aspect discussed briefly in Chapter 1 where it is pointed out that in training for fat loss, the duration of an activity is more important than its intensity (page 29). The evidence for this is shown here in relation to amounts of energy used in walking, running or jogging at different speeds. Obviously as the pace increases so does energy use. However, note the times that are required to use up a certain amount of energy (say in a 100g bar of chocolate).

Energy used in walking and running at different speeds

	Speed mins. per mile	Energy use kcal per min.	Use of 500 kcal* mins.	or miles
Walking	20	4	125	6.2
Jogging	10	11	45.4	4.5
	9	14	35.7	3.9
	8	17	29.4	3.6
Running	7	19	26.3	3.7
	6	22	22.7	3.8
	5	25	20	4.0

*approx. energy in 100g chocolate bar

Except in the case of walking, very little extra time is required to use up the same amounts of energy while moving at a slower speed. It is also interesting to note the distances which must be covered at these speeds to use this amount of energy. Again there is little difference. In fact, there is a point between speeds of 7 and 8 minutes per mile where faster running means that *more* distance must be covered to use the same amount of energy. This means that at faster speeds, less energy is used to cover a set distance because of the shorter times spent running – the implication of this being that elite runners may use *less* energy in a marathon, than middle of the field runners!

Types of nutrients

Healthy eating habits play an important part in fitness, and a good diet must contain six types of nutrients in the correct amounts. Three of these types are used in major quantities, carbohydrate, fat and protein. Substantial amounts of a fourth material, fibre, are also required, although technically this is not a nutrient since it is not actually taken into the cells of the body. The other two classes of nutrient, vitamins and minerals, are required in much smaller amounts but are no less important to health and fitness. A seventh type of food stuff, alcohol, can also make up a significant proportion of the total energy intake. The major characteristics, functions and sources of these nutrients are described below.

Carbohydrate (energy value = 4 kcal per gram)
Description – Carbohydrates come in various forms, but for

practical purposes can be classed in two basic groups: *simple carbohydrates* are soluble sugars such as grape sugar (glucose), table sugar (sucrose) and milk sugar (lactose); *complex carbohydrates*, or 'polysaccharides' meaning 'many sugars', are long insoluble chains of sugars, such as plant starches and animal glycogens.

Functions – This is the most available energy supply for the body, and it is also the source that fuels intense activity. It is stored in limited amounts as glycogen in the liver and the individual muscles; estimates of the total body store of carbohydrate vary from 300–600g, equivalent to 1200–2400 kcals or about a day's total energy requirements (alternatively, there is just over an hour's continuous running in the carbohydrate stores of a pair of legs).

Sources – Simple carbohydrates are present in sweet substances like jams, confectionery, fruits etc. Complex carbohydrates are found in unrefined plant products like wholemeal bread, muesli, pasta, potatoes and root vegetables.

Comments – Simple carbohydrates are easily digested and rapidly absorbed into the bloodstream, but complex carbohydrates are considered to be nutritionally superior because their unrefined sources also supply greater amounts of fibre, vitamins and minerals.

Fat (energy value = 9 kcal per gram)

Description – Fats are made up of sub-units called *fatty* acids, and different fats contain different fatty acids. There are two types of fatty acid: the 'saturated' fatty acids (saturated with hydrogen) are characteristic of animal fats; 'unsaturated' fatty acids are found in plant fats and vegetable oils (an oil is simply a fat that is liquid at room temperature).

Functions – Fats are a very concentrated form of energy; an individual's total energy requirements for a week are equivalent to just 5 lb of fat. Fats also play other roles in cell structure, hormone synthesis etc., but these functions, though vital, utilise very small amounts of fat by comparison with those involved in energy storage.

Sources – Obvious sources of fat are all dairy products, red meats and cooking oils. However, many processed or 'convenience' foods also have high fat contents (fat improves texture, taste and keeping powers). Foods low in fat include chicken, whitefish and most plant foods, except nuts and processed foods (crisps, chips).

**Percentage of fat in various foodstuffs
(g fat per 100g edible weight)**

Foodstuff	% Fat	Foodstuff	% Fat
Double cream	48	Herring	18
Cheddar cheese	33	Salmon	8
Butter, marge	82	Whitefish	0
Egg	11	Vegetables	0
Bacon	38	Fruit	0
Ham	19	Crisps	36
Beef	11	Roasted peanuts	49
Chicken	4	Chocolate	30
Luncheon meat	27	Cakes	5–15
Black pudding	22	Fried chips	11
Sausage	24–32	Cocoa	21
		Coffee, tea	0

Comments – Unsaturated fats of plant origin are thought to be nutritionally less harmful than saturated fats. And in addition, three particular unsaturated fatty acids are known as the *essential fatty acids* (they are essential to body function and must be supplied in the diet). Therefore, a certain amount of fat, preferably of plant origin, is necessary. However, fats require a lot of oxygen in order that their energy can be released; they are thus poor sources of energy for sports activities where oxygen supplies are already at a premium. Also, the body has an extremely limited capacity for using fat for anything but energy. Therefore if energy requirements are being met by carbohydrate, any fat in the diet is simply stored as body fat. Thus, although a certain amount of dietary fat is necessary, high fat intakes should be avoided.

Protein (energy value = 4 kcal per gram)
Description – Proteins are long chains of sub-units called *amino acids*. Around 20 different amino acids are involved in protein structure, and different proteins have different combinations of amino acids.
Functions – The primary functions of protein are structural; these include not only obvious structural components like skin and muscles, but also all the machinery inside cells. However, proteins can also be broken down to supply energy.
Sources – Animal sources like meat and fish are richer in protein than are plant products; egg protein is considered to have the best balance of amino acids. Reasonably rich plant sources include pulses, like peas and beans. (As discussed

later, getting enough protein, even for training purposes, is rarely a problem in a Western diet.)

Comments – It used to be thought that animal proteins were 'better' than proteins from plant sources. But rather than the protein itself, it is really the amino acid sub-units that the body requires in order to construct its own particular proteins. In this respect, there is no general difference in protein quality between supplies from plants or animals. In one way, however, protein quality is important: there are eight *essential amino acids* (essential to body function and essential in the diet). In some plant proteins, one or other of these amino acids is lacking, but acceptable protein intakes can still be obtained from plant sources by a suitably varied diet of plant products. In terms of quantity of protein, it is calculated that present Western intakes of around 100g per day are about three times more than the body's structural needs.

Fibre (no energy value since it is not taken into the body proper)

Description – Fibre, or roughage, is simply the indigestible parts of plants.

Functions – Fibre is required for the gut to function properly. Since it is not digested itself, it gives solid bulk to the gut contents. It also adsorbs, and thus removes, potentially harmful materials from the gut.

Sources – Fibre generally consists of the outside parts of plants, like skins and husks. It occurs in much greater amounts in unrefined or unprocessed plant products.

Comments – Societies with a high amount of fibre in their diet seem to have a much lower incidence of intestinal and bowel disorders. Most authorities recommend that dietary fibre should be increased to around 30g per day (present average Western levels are 10–20g per day).

Vitamins (A, B group, C, D, E, K)

Description – Vitamins are not synthesised by the body itself, but are needed in very small amounts for particular functions. They have a great variety of chemical structure but can be classified into two groups according to their solubility properties. *Water-soluble vitamins* (C and the B group) cannot be stored in the body. Their water solubility means that excess amounts are simply excreted in the urine and the body thus needs daily supplies of these vitamins. The *fat-soluble vitamins*

(A, D, E, K) can be stored within the body. In fact, some can actually reach toxic levels and there have been deaths from vitamin A poisoning (an example of the fact that just because something is essential, more of it is not necessarily better).

Functions – Besides being involved in growth and development, vitamins also function in several processes of energy provision. Therefore, although they do not act as energy sources themselves, they are still important factors to the body's energy equation.

Sources – Relatively rich sources of particular vitamins, and the general types of processes that particular vitamins are involved in, are listed:

A – (processes of vision) liver, carrots, dairy products.
B – (energy processes and nerve function) meat, fish, dairy products.
C – (healing processes and infections) fresh fruits, potatoes.
D – (processes of teeth and bone formation) dairy products, action of sunlight on skin.
E – (processes of muscle function) grains, nuts, liver.
K – (processes of fat digestion) green vegetables, liver.

Comments – Questions about the 'best' amounts of vitamins are not easily answered. Many sports people regularly take vitamin supplements, even though nutritionists traditionally maintain that adequate amounts are obtained from a balanced diet of fresh foods. However, recent analyses of the hair, skin, nails etc. of sportsmen have suggested that individuals in hard training can be suffering from vitamin deficiency. Therefore, it may be that the nutritionally recommended doses, derived as they are from investigations of diseases and disorders due to low levels or complete absences of certain vitamins, are inappropriate for the optimal functioning of extremely active individuals. So bearing in mind the dangers associated with extreme doses of the fat-soluble vitamins, there is no harm in taking some form of supplementation, especially of the daily-required B group and C (at worst, this merely makes expensive urine).

Minerals (potassium, sodium, chloride; calcium, magnesium, phosphorous; iron)
Description – These are simply chemical elements, and required in extremely small amounts. They are often referred

to in general terms as 'electrolytes', as in 'electrolyte drinks' (the term electrolyte simply means that a solution of these substances can conduct an electric current). They are also sometimes loosely referred to as 'salts' – this is being used in the chemical sense, and it does not mean they are similar to table salt, which contains only the two elements sodium and chloride. There is also a group of so-called *trace elements*, which are required by the body in minute (trace) amounts and which include copper, zinc and fluoride (further examples of substances that are poisonous in excess).

Functions – It is impossible to assign exact and specific roles to individual mineral elements, but the general areas of involvement are indicated below.

Sources – Particularly rich sources of certain minerals are:

i.   potassium – bananas; sodium, chloride – table salt. These minerals are involved in the fluid balance of the body, and in nerve function.

ii. calcium, magnesium – milk. These function in bone metabolism and in muscle action.

iii. phosphorous – green vegetables. This has many functions, but is particularly important to energy processes.

iv. iron – liver, vegetables. This is the basis of the oxygen-carrying ability of the blood.

Comments – Females in hard training should probably supplement their diet with iron. Otherwise, the biggest single disruption to the mineral balance of the body occurs in sweating. Usually these losses are made up by the minerals in a normal diet. Even in changed circumstances of excessive sweating in a warmer climate, the body adjusts within a few days so that less minerals are lost in the sweat; during the period of adjustment, some sort of electrolyte drink can be taken. It is nowadays strongly recommended that extra table salt is not used; not only does this not represent the actual minerals that are lost in sweat, but excessive sodium is harmful.

Alcohol (energy value = 7 kcal per gram)
Besides its obvious intoxicating effects, alcohol represents a significant amount of calories (its energy value is second only to fat); at around 200 kcals each, a couple of pints of beer can make a significant contribution to a day's total calorie intake. However, the energy in alcohol is not primarily available to the muscles. Alcohol can only be metabolised by the

liver, so it represents an extremely rich source of 'non-fitness' calories.

Sources – As indicated in the table, there are various amounts of alcohol in different types of alcoholic drink. The amount taken into the bloodstream, however, is not simply related to the amount in the type of drink; the alcohol concentration of fortified wines is actually more readily absorbed than the greater concentrations of undiluted spirits.

Alcohol contents and energy levels of various drinks

Beverage	% Alcohol	Kcals
Beer, bitter	3–5	155–320 (pint)
lager	2–4	75–185
Wine, red	7–10	90 (glass)
white	7–10	75
Fortified wines (sherry, Martini)	12–15	75–100
Spirits	30–50	50–80 (measure)

Comments – Alcohol has various physiological effects. It is a strong diuretic (stimulates urination), and this results in a dehydrating effect on the body. With beer, the effect is minimised since the alcohol in two pints of beer results in the excretion of one pint of fluid; but the alcohol in two measures of spirits also results in the excretion of one pint of fluid; wines too cause this net loss of body fluid. Further, it is probably well known that the effects of alcohol are related to body size, and to the contents (or not) of the stomach. There is also a third factor. The ability of the body to detoxify alcohol varies throughout the daily cycle, and is lowest between midnight and 4 a.m. This is why late night drinking sessions not only cost sleep, but the subsequent alcohol content of the body remains higher for longer.

Diet and training

Differences of size and activity between individuals make it impossible to give general recommendations about total amounts of food required; the daily 1500 kcals that is suitable for a sedentary lifestyle can rise to 5000 kcals to support training demands. More can be said, however, about types of food. The balance of major nutrients in the average

Western diet is around 40–45% fat, 45–55% carbohydrate and 10–15% protein, and fitness could benefit from some adjustment of these proportions.

General principles of nutrition for training:

1. Fat intake should be reduced. Fat is not a significant energy source for most sports, and body fat is usually a positive hindrance to performance. Fat intake could with advantage be halved from the present levels in the average diet, simply by more careful consumption of the high fat foods listed previously.

2. Protein intake does not need to be increased. High protein intakes are not necessary for general training purposes. The present average levels of consumption are well in excess of requirements; in fact, much of the presently consumed (expensive) protein is simply used as energy. In the average diet about 100g of protein are consumed per day, whereas around 0.5g per kilogram of bodyweight are considered sufficient.

3. Carbohydrate intake should be increased. Level of sports performance is directly related to the level of carbohydrate in the muscle. Because of the muscle's limited storage capacity, performance becomes related to the level of carbohydrate in the diet. Recent analyses of samples from active sportsmen indicate (surprisingly) that their muscle glycogen levels are often consistently low – the demands of training are not being met by the supplies in the diet. Therefore during hard training, carbohydrate intake should be increased, perhaps as much as doubling the intake of foods with high contents of the complex carbohydrates (cereals, potatoes, bread etc.).

4. The timing of food intake in relation to training is important. The most effective build-up of muscle glycogen stores occurs within an hour of the depletion. Therefore, it is more useful to eat soon after activity rather than hours later. Conversely, it has already been pointed out in the section on the provision of muscle energy, that there is no need for, or benefit from, a high calorie snack immediately before a sports event.

Carbohydrate loading. The requirement for several days of dietary preparation for an event is illustrated by the 'carbohydrate loading' diet of marathon runners. In its original form, this was quite a rigorous preparation. About 6 days before the event the athlete goes on a fast 'bleed-out' run to deplete the muscle glycogen reserves; then follows 3 days of low car-bohydrate diet, accompanied by as near normal training as such a diet allows; the preparations are completed by 3 days on a high carbohydrate diet coupled to light training. The idea is to deplete the muscle glycogen levels so severely that in these final 3 days, the replenishment 'overshoots' to higher than normal levels. The effectiveness of the diet has never been fully established for all individuals, and most athletes nowadays follow a modified procedure of simply topping-up with high carbohydrate and light training for the final few days after a bleed-out run.

4

LOSS OF FITNESS

Fitness can be lost in two ways – through the effects of age, and through the effects of inactivity. However until relatively recently, as people became older they tended also to become more inactive. Therefore it may be that many of our present notions about the seeming effects of aging will have to be revised, as more is found out about the present growing population of still-active, older sports men and women.

Age and Fitness

High levels of physical activity seem to slow down some aspects of the aging process. For example, individuals who exercise regularly usually have lower blood pressures, less body fat, less inflexibility etc. However, striking though the effects of exercise can be, they act only to delay the aging process rather than to halt it, and fitness does inevitably decline with age. The different components of fitness, though, do not decline at the same rates.

(Before considering individual components of fitness and age, it is worth emphasising that any 'age-related decline in fitness' refers to individuals who have been exercising regularly throughout their lives. That is, previously-inactive individuals who only start exercising later in life can improve their fitness, and even 'reverse' many of the effects of (inactive) aging. And this happens to some extent, no matter how late in life exercise is actually started.)

Effects of age

Skill. This aspect of fitness is least affected by age, although of course, there are considerable differences between the decline in particular skills, depending upon how much physical effort they require. But if a skill requires little effort, and especially if it is what is called 'self-paced', (see below), the only reason for any decline at all is a lower level of motivation. (A self-paced activity is one in which the movements and responses are more or less determined by the individual, e.g. archery, weightlifting; this is distinct from an 'open' situation in which movements are responses to an opponent or, say, the flight of a ball.)

Strength and speed. These related components show the greatest rates of decline with age. They really decline continuously after the age of about 25, but the effects often seem to become most apparent between the ages of 40–50. At this time there is also usually a dramatic reduction in muscle protein. By the age of 65, the level of strength can be less than 70% of what it was at the age of 30.

Stamina. Decline in stamina seems to occur much more slowly, although this may simply be a reflection of the greater numbers of older people who are now, through the rise in popularity of running, taking part in endurance training. Even so, capacity to utilise oxygen, measured as VO_2max, can decline by as much as 20% between the ages of 25–60.

Suppleness. This could be considered to start declining from birth, as the connective tissues, tendons and ligaments thicken during normal growth. With appropriate stretching, these stiffening effects can be greatly minimised, and unlike strength, speed and stamina, improvement in suppleness can be continued well into old age. On the other hand, if it is not trained, loss of suppleness can be one of the most dramatic effects of aging. (And this disappearance is likely to be even more rapid under the influence of the repetitively stiffening movements of endurance training.)

Skinniness. Although this is commonly lost with age, it need not change at all – skinniness is the one aspect of fitness that can be absolutely maintained against Time. The common increase in body fat is simply due to lack of diet adjustment to take account of decreases in levels of activity and in rates of body metabolism; with increasing age, there is less growth and structural repair.

This last point, decreased capacity for repair, raises an aspect of aging that is indirectly related to fitness. Since their tissues are less elastic and resilient, older sports men and women are much more vulnerable to injury. And any injuries take much longer to heal; a muscle strain may heal within a week or 10 days in a young athlete, but require three to four weeks in an older individual.

Training recommendations for increasing age:

1. More, rather than less, attention should be paid to all aspects of fitness. Games players who are still active after the age of about 30 usually realise that more, rather than less, training is required to maintain performance. The same point applies to all aspects of general fitness – increasing age requires a more deliberate and conscious effort to reach or maintain certain standards of fitness.

2. More attention should be paid to diet. Less energy is used with increasing age, and body fat tends to accumulate unnoticed.

3. Endurance activities should be carried out. These are the kinds of activities that are of the greatest general benefit. They control weight, have beneficial effects on the heart and cardio-respiratory system, and build local endurance in the legs.

4. Particular attention should be paid to suppleness. Not only should specific stretching exercises be carried out, but it is also useful to engage in other types of activity (perhaps self-paced, like swimming) to help counteract the unsuppling effects of any repetitive endurance training.

5. Strength training is of benefit. Notwithstanding the inevitable decline in strength with age, some sort of strength training programme should be carried out, particularly for upper body fitness. This also has positive effects on flexibility and muscle tone. (Exercise machines like the multigym may be more suitable for older individuals since they place less stress on the joints and the back.)

Inactivity and Fitness

When a broken limb is eventually released from its plaster cast, its wasted appearance dramatically illustrates the effects of inactivity. The basic point to be quite clear about is that virtually all aspects of fitness decline during inactivity; the only differences are that some decline slowly and others disappear quickly.

Effects on different components of fitness

Skill. This aspect again shows one of the slowest rates of decline during inactivity, and any decline that does occur can be corrected much more quickly than the skill was originally acquired. Also, the extent of decline is influenced by the way in which the skill was originally acquired; a skill is likely to be retained better if it has been developed in many short practice sessions, rather than in more concentrated but fewer sessions. However, the problem is that most sports skills require a certain amount of strength and stamina for their expression, and these components of fitness show a more rapid deterioration than skill itself.

Strength and speed. Strength is lost relatively quickly. Decreases in muscle size have been detected after as little as 36 hours of inactivity, and a measurable decline in strength after three days. In a trained individual, strength can decrease by as much as 25% during two weeks of inactivity. Inborn speed may not be greatly affected by inactivity, but its expression in most sports is highly dependent on strength, so actual speed can also show considerable deterioration.

Stamina. The rate of decline in stamina is generally a bit slower than that of strength. The situation here is complicated by the different rates of deterioration of the individual components of stamina. Most features of heart function, such as stroke volume and rate of beat, show little change over weeks of inactivity (presumably any body activity at all during this period still contributes something towards the maintenance of heart performance). But the VO_2max can decline by as much as 20% within three to four weeks, indicating that other aspects of the aerobic system deteriorate fairly rapidly. These include decreases in the capillary network of the lungs and in the total blood volume of the body. Local changes also occur at the level of the muscles; the energy-processing machinery in the muscle degenerates, and the training-enhanced network of capillaries is also progressively closed down if no demands are made on them. Effects of training on local muscular endurance seem to be completely lost within six weeks of inactivity.

Suppleness. This can actually increase, at least during the early stages of a period of inactivity. Unexercised muscles tend to lengthen and to lose their tone and density; connective tissues, tendons and ligaments also decrease in thickness and density. All this simply contributes towards a 'looser' framework. (Inactive individuals are thus often much more supple than physically active people – stomachs and body fat permitting!)

Skinniness. This, of course, can show a rapid deterioration. The rate and final extent of deterioration are directly related to the food intake, and the end results of seemingly trivial (but regular) imbalances of the body's energy equation can be quite dramatic – the unused energy per day, equivalent merely to two pints of beer (420 kcals), would put on about 3 lb of fat in a month.

Thus fitness is not something that can be stored for use at some future date. If it is not being developed, it is being lost – and in general, it is lost at a much faster rate than it is gained. An individual is only as fit as the previous day's training session.

Injury and Fitness

Injury and fitness are very closely related – anyone who does a reasonable amount of training has probably already been injured, and in all likelihood is going to become injured again. Therefore in a book about fitness, it may be useful to say something about injury. However, this is not a medical account, nor is it intended as a guide for self-diagnosis. The aims here are simply to outline the common types of injuries and their causes in order that they can be avoided, to indicate what to do about injury if it does occur, and to suggest how to cope with injury in relation to maintaining fitness.

Nuisance conditions

Some states are probably regarded more as nuisances rather than as injuries, but they are disabling and sometimes can be painful enough to prevent training completely. The most common conditions of this nature are: colds, cramp, muscle stiffness and a stitch.

Colds, flu. Many experienced people continue to train during a cold, and claim that this helps recovery. Conversely, individuals with cold symptoms have actually died while training or competing. So, light activity may be continued during a cold, but with the awareness that cold symptoms can also result from other types of infection. And no serious training should be carried out if there is any temperature or headache. Before re-starting training after flu or a fever, the same number of symptom-free days should be allowed for recovery, as the symptoms lasted for; if the symptoms lasted two days, a further two days should be allowed before re-starting training.

Cramp. This results from muscles going into spasm. It can arise during prolonged activity or be unassociated with activity, and is generally due to an imbalance of minerals (electrolytes) in the muscles (note, not a deficiency of 'salt' – opinion nowadays is against taking salt tablets). Cramp is relieved simply by stretching the muscle against the cramping tendency. Some advance preparation against cramp might be provided by bananas or dried apricots (rich in potassium and magnesium), although if cramp is persistent, medical advice should be sought.

Stiffness. There are two categories of muscle stiffness, both of which can be quite painful. That associated with major muscle injury is considered later. Here we are concerned with the stiffness that sometimes results from exercise. This used to be thought to arise from the build-up of lactic acid, but is nowadays considered to be due to numerous tiny muscle tears and fluid accumulation caused by activity of an unaccustomed type or intensity. The remedy is simply more activity. Some stretching immediately after any intense activity, and again a few hours later, can minimise subsequent stiffness. Care should be taken in working off this type of stiffness in case it hides a more serious injury; if a particular area of stiffness hasn't eased after 10 minutes of gentle exercise, it should be viewed with suspicion.

Stitch. The basis of this sharp pain in the side is not really known. Suggestions range from trapped internal gases, through cramp in the diaphragm muscle, to irritation of ligaments that attach to the diaphragm. There are also many different suggested causes of stitch, from exercising too soon after eating, exercising too long after eating, breathing too shallowly, running downhill, or having the internal organs continuously jolted. What is more clear is that it is brought about by, or is a symptom of, stress, and that certain individuals are more prone to stitch. Its remedy simply consists of reducing the level of activity until the stitch disappears. Relief can often be hastened by expelling each breath very forcefully for a few minutes (sometimes a stitch goes away during the heavy breathing and forward leaning of running uphill).

Common injury treatments
There are several self-help treatments which can be useful.

Common sense. The application of this is one of the most important treatments, especially realising when to stop exercise, when to start again and how much to do. Continuing a match, or returning too early to full training, can be costly in terms of subsequent further delay.

Cold. Cooling the affected part is one of the most generally used, and effective, treatments. This should be done immediately in the case of sudden soft tissue injuries like sprains or muscle strains, where it minimises any internal bleeding or swelling. It is also useful in relieving pain that appears after a training activity, e.g. runner's shin soreness, or in the early stages of injury rehabilitation where there is sometimes pain after an exercise session. The cooling treatment should only be carried out for a limited length of time, continuous application for periods longer than 15–20 minutes can result in greater subsequent pain and stiffness. Various cooling agencies can be used. Ice itself should be wrapped in a cloth rather than being applied directly to the skin. A cold water tap or a stream can also be useful. And many sports people keep a (suitably marked) packet of frozen peas in the freezer for injury purposes, since these mould round limbs better than lumps of ice.

I.C.E. These letters indicate the complete treatment of acute injury – ice, compression, elevation. When the ice has been removed, a compression bandage should be applied to minimise any swelling from a flush of blood into the previously cooled area (not overtight, of course, and an eye should be kept on the parts beyond the strapping for any numbness or signs of restricted blood flow). The 'elevation' consists of resting the injured part in a raised position, above the level of the heart if possible, again to minimise swelling.

Heat. The local application of gentle heat by damp towels or hot water bottles relaxes stiff muscles and stimulates the circulation. This is a good treatment for muscle strains, *after* the post-injury 24–48 hour recovery period.

Contrast bathing. This consists of alternating cold and hot treatments. The injured part is treated with water as hot as can be tolerated, then with ice water; each treatment lasts for about a minute, through a complete session of 5 or 6 cycles of hot and cold, ending with hot. Basins can be used for the hands and feet, but more awkward areas can be treated with wet towels. The treatment is thought to act through an internal massaging or flushing effect, by alternately constricting and dilating the circulatory system. It should be carried out several times a day, and is effective in reducing pain and swelling in ligament and tendon injuries.

Epsom salts. An old remedy for strains and sprains is to wrap the injury in a bandage soaked in a strong solution of 'veterinary strength' Epsom salts (magnesium sulphate). This often relieves pain in a deeper injury.

Professional treatments

Other treatments that are used by professionally qualified individuals include: *ultrasound*, which uses sound waves to produce mechanical vibrations and heat effects within tissues (a sort of very vigorous internal micro-massage); *shortwave diathermy*, which is a form of radiation that produces strong heating effects deep within tissues; and various forms of massage, and joint and spine manipulation.

Common sports injuries

The more common types of injuries that can occur during training or have a disruptive effect on fitness, are described below in alphabetical order according to the common name for the injury; the causes and general types of treatment for each injury are also indicated.

Blister (skin)
Basis – Separation of the skin layers and accumulation of fluid from damaged cells.
Cause – Local heating effects due to friction (feet blisters are more likely when running in hot weather).
Treatment – Burst with a sterile needle and cover with adhesive tape.
Comments – Blood blisters represent more severe damage but are treated similarly. **Black toe-nails** are due to the accumulation of blood under the nail and result from ill-fitting shoes which squash the toes during activity; usually no treatment is required and in severe cases the nail drops off in a month or so. If an already black nail becomes very painful, it usually means that another blister has formed beneath it, and a surgery visit may be necessary.

Bruise (any tissue with a blood supply; skin, muscle, tendon, bone membrane)
Basis – Rupture of small blood capillaries.
Cause – Direct blow that does not break the skin.
Treatment – Immediate application of cold to limit internal bleeding.
Comments –Subsequent exercise can help to disperse the accumulated blood; in severe cases, a bruise may need to be dispersed under medical advice by heat, massage or the application of hyaluronidase and heparinoid ointments (these are blood anti-coagulants). Different people show different tendencies for bruising, depending on the fragility of their blood capillaries.

Bursitis (joints; shoulder, knee, elbow, ankle)
Basis – Bursae are fluid-filled sacs that ease the movement of adjacent tissues against each other, and are present where skin, muscles or tendons rub over bones (elbow, knee, ankle) and in joints (shoulder). A bursa can become inflamed, with visible but fairly harmless swelling (housemaid's knee), or be more deep-seated and painful (around the Achilles tendon of the ankle).

bursa

Fig. 4 Housemaid's knee.

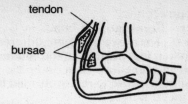

**Fig. 5 Inflamed bursae of
the Achilles tendon.**

Cause – Inflammation through over-use or repeated pressure.
Treatment – Rest, anti-inflammatory drugs.

Cartilage problems (usually of the knee)
Basis – There are two sorts of cartilage. In most limb joints,
the ends of the bones are covered with protective articular
cartilage; this can flake off and cause pain in, or even locking
of, the joint. The knee also has another type of cartilage, the
menisci, which are fibrous pads that may aid smooth movement; these cartilage pads can become squashed or damaged.
Cause – Wear and tear in the joint, causing flaking. Sudden
twisting of the joint, causing pad damage.
Treatment – None, or surgery.
Comments – Cartilage problems commonly develop in games
players whose legs are subjected to severe twisting movements. Runners are more likely to develop the condition of
the knee that is described next.

Chondromalacia of the kneecap
Basis – Pain directly under the kneecap, especially during
running itself, walking downstairs, or even after prolonged
sitting.
Cause – It is thought to be due to the kneecap 'tracking'
wrongly during movement, and may arise from weakness in
the quadriceps muscles just above the knee.
Treatment – If knee movement is actually painful, the appropriate muscles can still be exercised by twitching the kneecap,
or by sitting on the floor and raising the leg with the knee
kept locked in the straight position.
Comments – The muscles above the knee help to hold the
kneecap in place, but are only brought wholly into play when
the knee is fully straight. Since the leg is never fully
straightened in distance running, these muscles can become
quite weak if the runner covers a high mileage – thus the
importance for runners of straight leg lifts and full leg extensions on the multigym.

Fracture (bone)

Basis – Breakage of a bone.

Cause – There are two quite different causes. Acute fractures (a broken leg) arise from the sudden imposition of force, and result in immediate pain and local swelling. **Stress fractures** occur in response to relatively mild but repetitive force, rather like metal fatigue.

Treatment – Cessation of activity; usually limb immobilisation for an acute fracture, and rest with or without strapping for a stress fracture (4–6 weeks).

Comments – Stress fractures usually show a gradual onset of pain over some weeks, and are difficult to diagnose; often the line of fracture doesn't show up on X-ray until a certain amount of healing bone growth has occurred along it. Any chronic pain in a bony area (feet, ankles, shins), particularly if it is only on one limb, should be viewed with suspicion.

Sciatica (sciatic or spinal nerve)

Basis – Irritation of the spinal nerve, resulting in pain in any place from the lower back, through the buttocks and thighs, even right down the leg to the foot.

Cause – A damaged disc or joint of the spine places pressure on a nerve root; it can occur suddenly while lifting, or have a gradual onset.

Treatment – Rest. In mild cases, stretching exercises can be helpful (hanging from a bar; slow, trunk-twisting movements in a seated position).

Comments – This condition, of course, is not solely associated with sport. It is included mainly to allow distinction to be made between it and pain due to hamstring injury at the rear of the thigh. In hamstring injury, the onset of pain is sudden. A sciatic condition is usually characterised by a sporadic or gradual onset of pain, often during prolonged sitting, and often in different parts of the leg.

Sprain (joints, especially ankle, knee, wrist, thumb)

Basis – Stretching or actual tearing of the connective ligaments that support a joint; blood capillaries are also usually affected, resulting in swelling and bruising; the muscles around the joint may also be damaged.

Cause – Sudden twisting of the joint, giving immediate swelling.

Treatment – Immediate treatment consists of limiting the swelling by I.C.E. Subsequent treatment consists of continued inactivity, with contrast bathing to reduce the swelling. Mobilising activities should be started when most of the swelling has gone down (bruising may still be present). Load-bearing activity should not be started until the joint is pain-free and fully mobile.

Comments – Sprained ligaments can take weeks, or even months, to heal. Ligaments that have been badly stretched no longer support their joint, and usually some strapping is required during training for a considerable time after the injury (such strapping is necessary, and is not 'weakening' the joint).

Strain (muscle, tendon; 'pulled muscle')

Basis – Sudden tearing of muscle fibres or of the muscle tendon; usually there is also rupture of blood capillaries resulting in bruising, inflammation and swelling. The tear can extend right through the muscle, or more usually, involve only a limited number of fibres. Such partial tears can occur within the muscle *(intramuscular tears)*, or be confined to the muscle surface *(interstitial tears)*; an intramuscular tear is generally more swollen and tender due to the unrelieved pressure within the muscle; an interstitial tear is usually less painful, though the discolouration due to the release of blood into the surface tissues may be spectacular.

Cause – A blow while the muscle is contracting, or simply the sudden application of force.

Treatment – Immediate treatment consists of minimising bleeding by I.C.E. Later treatment is concerned with maximising recovery by stimulating the circulation to remove waste products. The rate of recovery depends on the degree of damage. After a fairly severe tear, the muscle should be kept as inactive as possible for two days; the circulation can be stimulated by gentle heat on the third day; it is also important to begin gentle stretching and non-loadbearing exercise around this point; by about 10 days, more active exercise can be explored. While it is important that the muscle receives some gentle exercise during this 10 day recovery period, it should be borne in mind that any pain probably means that it is being damaged further.

Comments – Damaged muscle tissue can regenerate itself to a certain extent. However, the major repair processes involve laying down non-muscle connective fibres. These scar tissues are strong but relatively inextensible, and this is why it is important to begin stretching a torn muscle early in the recovery period. Scar tissues can continue to be laid down for a considerable period, so stretching should be continued for a month or so after injury.

Tendinitis (tendons; forearm, ankle, shoulder)
Basis – Irritation and swelling of a tendon (the tissue that connects muscle to bone), resulting in tenderness and painful stiffness, especially in the mornings.
Cause – Over-use, stretching or actual pressure on the tendon. Pain in the Achilles tendon can affect a novice, or an experienced runner who increases road mileage too suddenly; it can also arise from pressure of the high tabs at the rear of many training shoes.
Treatment – Rest or reduction in activity, with gentle stretching; ultrasound or contrast bathing may reduce the inflammation.
Comments – Tendon damage is the basis of such conditions as tennis elbow (outer side of elbow) and golfer's elbow (inner side). In some places, a tendon is covered with a membrane or passes through a protective sheath; these coverings themselves can become irritated, to result in conditions known respectively as **peritendinitis** and **tenosynovitis**, in which the tendon no longer slides painlessly back and forward (if the fingers are placed lightly on the painful area, an actual crackling or grating sensation can often be felt during movement).

Responses to injury
Injuries fall into two general categories in regard to their rates of onset and the sorts of treatments or responses that they require. On the one hand, acute (sudden) injuries occur instantaneously as a result of some single incident, either external (a blow) or internal (a muscle tear). Although such immediate injuries are always painful and often serious, they are relatively straightforward in terms of cause, diagnosis and treatment. On the other hand, chronic (over-use) injuries develop more slowly as a result of repeated incidents. The gradual onset of these injuries, often in the seeming absence of any particular cause, makes them much more troublesome to diagnose and treat.

Responses to acute injury
Immediate treatment in this type of injury is aimed at minimising damage, internal bleeding and swelling. If this is not carried out, subsequent recovery time is often required

not so much for repair of the actual injury itself as for clearing up the after-effects of internal bleeding. (It should be emphasised that the situations considered in this section do not include medical emergencies. Any serious injuries, especially head injuries or cases of unconsciousness, should be immediately referred to a Casualty Department.)

Reponses to acute soft tissue injury (muscle strains, joint sprains):

1. Stop activity. Completing a run or a training session after an injury has occurred is profitless. Such a single period of training has little effect in improving fitness, but is likely to have a large effect in damaging fitness, through the subsequent longer lay-off that it causes.

2. Cool the affected area. The ideal situation is the application of I.C.E. Other cooling agencies should be kept in mind (water tap, stream). The application of pressure can also be makeshift; on the games field, an effective treatment for a severe blow on the thigh is immediate application of very forceful thumb pressure directly over the injury for about a minute (more effectively carried out by someone else, since it is fairly painful).

3. Continue the inactivity, pressure bandage and elevation for 24–48 hours. At this point it is time to decide whether medical help is required. This really depends on the nature and severity of the injury, and on past personal experience.

4. Start rehabilitation exercise as soon as possible. Sports medicine authorities nowadays recommend an early start to rehabilitative exercise. The full sequence of rehabilitation is described later in this section. Briefly, it involves: within 3–4 days of a muscle injury, beginning gentle non-loadbearing stretching; and as soon as most of the swelling has gone down in a joint sprain, beginning non-loadbearing mobilising exercise.

Responses to chronic pains

Pain is Nature's way of saying something is wrong, and of trying to prevent further damaging activity. The progressive development of pain signals the onset of an over-use injury, usually to the tissues of bone, ligaments or tendons, and most often in the feet, ankles, shins, knees or wrists.

Response to over-use injuries:

1. Stop activity. In this type of injury, over-activity is the general cause of the condition, so, rather than an early start to any rehabilitative exercise, a period of rest is the general form of response.

2. Identify the cause of the condition. Every injury, even one of so-called over-use, has a particular cause, and it is important to determine this, to prevent it from happening again. A training diary can be of great help here, with its record of forgotten twists, falls, intense training sessions, new training methods, new shoes etc.

3. Decide whether outside help is required. Any injury that is painful enough to interfere with training, and which a week's rest hasn't helped, probably requires professional attention. However, a doctor's surgery may not be the best first stop, especially if the doctor is not sports-oriented. (Sympathy is unlikely to be forthcoming if the symptoms only occur while lifting a weight or after a five mile run.) In the absence of a Sports Injury Clinic, help with a chronic injury can often be obtained from individuals who are engaged in the same activity that caused the condition – the appropriate local sports club. At least they may suggest a physiotherapist, chiropodist or osteopath who helped someone else with similar symptoms.

Of course, actually dealing with or making decisions about an injury is not always as straightforward as the above suggestions imply. The sorts of questions and answers outlined below may help in planning a course of action.

Questionnaire for dealing with chronic injuries and niggling pains:

1. Does it interfere with the intensity, duration or regularity of training?

a) **answer** – no; **response** – ignore it, there is no problem (at least for training and fitness).

b) **answer** – no, but it becomes more painful during or after training;

          response – try cooling, immediately after a training session (this situation will probably soon resolve itself into either answer (a) or answer (c).

c) **answer** – yes; **response** – training of the injured part should cease (fitness is declining anyway, but the injury is still being aggravated; a week's break may settle the injury with less loss of fitness than 3 weeks' poor training).

2. Is the condition improved after 5 to 7 days of rest?

a) **answer** – yes; **response** – cautiously resume training; ensure a *graduated* build-up of activity for the injured part; *and answer question 3.*

b) **answer** – no; **response** – seek help (local Sports Clinic or enquire at an appropriate sports club).

3. What caused the condition?

a) site of an old injury?

b) lack of adequate warm-up or stretching routines?

c) a forgotten fall, twist, stumble etc?

d) new training equipment (especially shoes)? *or* very old shoes?

e) new training programme or a recent unusual activity, e.g.

new conditions (new route, new terrain)?

unusually heavy training session (intensity or duration)?

rapid increase in training load?

unusual activity (new game or sport)?

Rehabilitation from injury

The stages in rehabilitation of an injury are outlined below. It is difficult to generalise about the timing of the different phases, but pain can act as a useful guide. The general rule is that some pain after exercise is normal, but pain during the exercise is probably doing further damage. Therefore, if pain gets worse, or appears earlier during the exercise, or causes the movement to become more restricted, then the rate of progression is too rapid.

Progression in injury rehabilitation:

1. 24–48 hours inactivity, compression, elevation;

2. stimulation of circulation – local heat, contrast bathing, *gentle* massage;

3. mobilisation – isometric contractions, non-loadbearing activity (circling movements, movements in a swimming pool);

4. initial activity – supported 'negative only' movements, before positive, loaded movements are attempted;

5. training activity when a full range of pain-free movement is
   possible.

Training during injury

Many sports men and women treat a period of injury as a
period of inactivity. However, an injury to one body part
need not be a reason (or excuse) for total inactivity – in fact,
far from being an idle time, a period of injury is fairly busy
since general fitness must be maintained somehow, and the
injury must be rehabilitated.

Training priorities during injury:

1. If necessary, adjust the general level of diet. Skinniness is
one aspect of fitness that should be maintained. The extent to
which the diet needs adjustment depends, of course, on the
degree of activity that can be maintained. But a complete cessation of training could well represent a saving of 1000 kcals
a day that the body will store somewhere as fat, at about 1.5 lb
per week.

2. If possible, maintain some activity of the injured part. Besides
rehabilitation of the actual site of injury, the body part in which
the injury is located should be kept as active as possible: if a
foot is injured, exercise that leg; if a calf is injured, exercise
that thigh; if the thigh is injured, exercise that calf and ankle.
The purpose of this is to minimise muscle deterioration and to
keep the blood capillaries open. The selectivities of weight training exercises are useful here, particularly on supportive training
machines like a multigym.

3. Maintain cardiorespiratory fitness. Since the cardiorespiratory
system is exercised by any activity that raises the heart and
breathing rates, this aspect of fitness can be maintained in
various ways. Cycling and swimming are both relatively non-
stressful on joints, but both must be carried out at greater than
'recreational' intensities to have useful training effects. Modified
circuit training is also useful.

4. Deliberately improve some other aspect of fitness. It is important to maintain a positive attitude during depressing periods
of injury, and this can often be helped by using an injury as an
opportunity to develop some other aspect of fitness – a broken
leg is simply Nature's way of suggesting that you need some
upper body work!

Index